SELECTIONS FROM JUSTIN MARTYR'S
DIALOGUE WITH TRYPHO

Published in the United States in 1964 by

ASSOCIATION PRESS

291 Broadway, New York City, New York

The series World Christian Books is sponsored by
the Commission on World Mission and Evangelism
of the World Council of Churches. This volume,
under the same title, was published in Great Britain
by the United Society for Christian Literature
(Lutterworth Press, London) in 1963.

Price $1.25

*Printed in Great Britain
by Page Bros. (Norwich) Limited, Mile Cross Lane, Norwich*

WORLD CHRISTIAN BOOKS NO. 49

Third Series

Selections from
JUSTIN MARTYR'S DIALOGUE
WITH
TRYPHO, A JEW

translated and edited by

R. P. C. HANSON

ASSOCIATION PRESS, NEW YORK

First Series:

Second Series:

Third Series:

NOTE

Quotations from the Old Testament in this work have all been placed in italics; as they are quotations from the Greek version of the Old Testament, called the Septuagint, sometimes they differ from the English versions, which are based on the Hebrew text; in cases where the differences are marked, the reference has after it in brackets the conventional abbreviation for the Septuagint, thus: (LXX). Clear quotations from the New Testament have not been put in italics, but the references have been given; in many cases it is impossible to assign an exact New Testament text to Justin's New Testament quotations because he was relying on his memory or on some source which conflated or mixed quotations from the Synoptic gospels; an attempt has been made to indicate where this is the case. It has proved impossible, in the process of reducing Justin's 58,000 Greek words to 20,000 English words, to do justice to all the facets of his thought. All that is attempted here is a presentation in small compass by means of selection of the main course of his argument and the main points of his thought. The text translated is that presented by E. J. Goodspeed in pp. 90-265 of his *Die Ältesten Apologeten* (Göttingen 1914). The useful and accurate translation of the *Dialogue* made by A. Lukyn Williams (London 1930), furnished with valuable notes, has been extensively drawn upon for assistance and comparison, but the translation is entirely my own.

R.P.C.H.

TABLE OF THE PASSAGES OF THE *DIALOGUE* TRANSLATED

INTRODUCTION

I

Justin who wrote the *Dialogue with Trypho* was born about A.D. 100 in Neapolis (now Nablus), the ancient Shechem, in Palestine. He regarded himself as a Samaritan, but he was not a Jew by race; he had not, for instance, been circumcised. On the other hand, it is quite clear from his works, and especially from the *Dialogue*, that he was well informed about the Judaism which was contemporary with him. Almost all the opinions which he attributes to Rabbinic teachers and the statements which he makes about Jews in the *Dialogue* can be confirmed as accurate from other sources. It was no doubt because he knew himself to be particularly well-informed about the Jews that he felt qualified to write such a work as the *Dialogue*. His spiritual and intellectual pilgrimage towards Christianity is described by himself in this work (caps.2-8). He does not give the impression of having studied any philosophy very carefully except that of Plato, and even here what he says about Platonism does not necessarily imply a profound knowledge of it. He speaks cavalierly and almost derisively of other philosophies, in this maintaining the tradition of several apologists of the second and third centuries (e.g. Tatian, Hermias, Minucius Felix, Tertullian). He certainly regarded himself as a philosopher however; Trypho's greeting to him, "Hullo, philosopher!" was a quite appropriate one. He is recorded as having spent the last part of his life from at latest 150 onwards teaching as a Christian philosopher, wearing the conventional philosopher's cloak, in a hired lodging in Rome. Two more of his works survive, both of them written before the *Dialogue*: the *First Apology*, a defence of Christianity addressed to the Emperor Antoninus Pius, and published probably between 150 and 154, and the *Second Apology*, which is a mere brief appendix to the first, and may have appeared two years later than it. His *Dialogue* probably appeared about 161. One of Justin's pupils, Tatian, wrote an apology himself, in which he referred in tones of the warmest admiration to Justin.

Justin was martyred in Rome at some point between 163 and

167, for professing Christianity. It was doubtless on the information of a rival philosopher, a pagan, called Crescens, to whom he refers in his *Second Apology*, that he was arrested. Tatian also mentions in his apology Crescens' hostility to Justin. An account of the martyrdom of Justin and his companions, which is generally reckoned to be trustworthy, has come down to us[1]. Among those who are strictly to be described as early Christian apologists (i.e. excluding Tertullian, who was much more than an apologist) none has left us more works than Justin. Christian posterity paid him the compliment not only of preserving his two most important works, but of forging several others in his name.

II

If the *Dialogue with Trypho* was written about 160 and the actual discussion with Trypho took place during or shortly after the Jewish war which ended in 135, it is unlikely that it represents precisely the actual words, or even the actual course, of the discussion. But there is no reason to think that some discussion did not take place between Justin and a Jew. Trypho's arguments are not simply the answers of one who is there to give the principal character cues for his speeches. He argues as a Jew of his day would have argued, though there are parts of the *Dialogue* where he appears to have been virtually forgotten. It is difficult to believe, too, that a Jewish antagonist could have remained calm in face of the unfair accusations which Justin makes against the whole Jewish race in the latter part of the *Dialogue*. There was a well-known Rabbi Tarphon who flourished between 90 and 130 A.D., and who was known as a particularly bitter opponent of Jewish Christians. It is not impossible that he may have been the person who had the original argument with Justin. If so, Justin must have considerably sweetened Tarphon's replies in the *Dialogue*. But this alteration of a dialogue in the process of presenting it for publication was not unknown in the ancient world, and would have been regarded as quite a normal and legitimate device.

The *Dialogue* is not very tidily arranged. There is a good deal of repetition, and during the last few chapters Justin appears to have thought of a number of miscellaneous objections and points which

[1] A translation of it is included in the volume *Faithful Witnesses* in the World Christian Books Series.

8

he should have included earlier. But there is a general pattern visible which, it is hoped, the headings under which the material translated has been divided will make clear. Once Justin's premises have been accepted, the argument is reasonably orderly and reasonably cogent. The style begins by being fresh and vigorous and true to life, but as the argument develops it alters and becomes looser and more hurried and tends to lapse into a string of untidily arranged clauses. It is as if Justin felt that he must hastily push on with his task, as the time during which he would be at liberty to write might be very short.

III

Justin's argument in the *Dialogue with Trypho* was not a new one. The main lines of his case are as follows: Christ was the embodiment in human form of a divine being who had existed from of old with God the Father; his activity can be discerned in innumerable passages in the Old Testament; every move and every word of his earthly career had been predicted in detail in the Old Testament; and these predictions, taken together with the effect which the Christian Church was having upon the minds and bodies of men and women throughout the contemporary Roman Empire, constituted irresistible evidence for the truth of Christianity. These were also the main lines of the case of every Christian who wrote a defence of Christianity in the second and third centuries; even of men who were very much greater theologians than Justin, like Tertullian and Origen. Justin differs from the other apologists strictly so called (i.e. excluding Tertullian and Origen) by paying much more attention to the actual details of Jesus' earthly life and by keeping well in view the life and practice of the Church, and in particular the sacraments of Baptism and Holy Communion.

In presenting his Old Testament proof-texts — which constitute, after all, the great bulk of the material of the *Dialogue* — Justin was drawing upon a great stock of proof-texts against the Jews which were widely current in the early Church and which had been used by several authors before Justin's day (some of them writers of the New Testament), and which were to be used by many writers of Christian argument after Justin's day. Indeed the use of the proof-text (a practice itself borrowed from the Jews, perhaps directly from the Qumran Covenanters who used the literature of the Dead Sea

9

Scrolls) was the normal Christian method of interpreting the Scriptures until Origen's genius popularized the commentary, a literary form which he had borrowed from the Gnostics.

We do not know where Justin got his doctrine of the Person of Christ. For him, as for all the apologists proper, Christ is a divine being, *now* different in number from the Father, i.e. enjoying a separate individual existence as a divine being; but he clearly believes (as did Irenaeus and Tertullian after him) that Christ *originally* was the reason or wisdom of God, or a power of God, residing unseparated with God's being and not yet enjoying individual existence. When God created the world and wished to communicate with it, with men, and particularly with God's chosen race, the Jews, this reason or wisdom or power became a separate, individual being. It was consciously put forth by God, but without in any sense dividing God or making Him less than before. Jesus Christ was this divine being become incarnate by being born as a man through the Blessed Virgin Mary. Did Justin learn this doctrine from the Fourth Gospel? We must not assume unreflectingly that he did. In the first place, it is far from certain that Justin accepted the Fourth Gospel as being on a level with the other three. When he wrote, this Gospel had not yet won full recognition as worthy to be ranked with the other three; his references to it are fewer and obscurer than his references to the first three; and though he often in both *Dialogue* and *Apology* refers to the "memoirs of the apostles", he never uses this phrase of a quotation which can be traced to the Fourth Gospel. In the second place, Justin's Christology is not exactly the Christology of the Fourth Gospel. Justin thinks of a Word or Reason (*Logos*) who was first within the being of God the Father and then, for purposes of creation, became a separate individual divine being. This is not the teaching of the Fourth Gospel. The most we can say is that Justin and the early apologists derived their Christology from circles and sources which were speculating about the concept of a divine Word or Reason (*Logos*), but that Justin's thought on this subject took a different line from that followed by the Fourth Gospel.

IV

In interpreting the Bible Justin uses the methods of his own time. These are methods that we cannot rightly use now. Justin

10

assumes that any verse—any half-verse—can legitimately be torn from its context and divorced from its historical background, and he applies such verses directly, often by the most far-fetched interpretation, to Christ or the Church. Moreover, he believes that the Septuagint version is absolutely accurate, and sometimes prefers it to the original Hebrew. Even by the critical standards of his own day, he ought to have known better than this. He assumes, too, that all the sins of the people of Israel, which they themselves had so honestly chronicled in their own Scriptures, could be directly attributed to the Jews of the first century A.D. We have to admit that this unchristian view was often taken by the Christian Church when it persecuted the Jews in later times.

In Justin's defence, however, it must be said that his attitude to the Old Testament was almost exactly the same as that of the Jews of his day. It was indeed from Judaism that Christians had inherited their attitude to the Scriptures. This accounts for Trypho's apparent helplessness before Justin's sometimes quite unfair attack. And it is because of this, too, that the *Dialogue* is so valuable historically. It gives us an incomparable picture of Christians and Jews interpreting the Bible early in the history of the Christian Church. Justin's treatment of the New Testament is also very instructive and interesting. He clearly values it highly—such of it as he knows—as first-rate historical information about Jesus and his apostles. But he does not regard it as Holy Scripture on a level with the Jewish Scriptures, nor as inspired, as his often-repeated phrase, "the memoirs of the apostles", shows.

What we cannot agree with in Trypho's objections is his inability to see that the Messiah might deliberately allow himself to be crucified, and that this might be according to the will of God. Here Justin wins our sympathy, rather than in his elaborate attempts to twist the Old Testament into a series of oracular predictions about the earthly life of Christ. He accepted whole-heartedly that the cross was at the centre of the Christian faith, that salvation means faith in the crucified and risen Jesus, who really was man, with the weaknesses and limitations of men. And the title by which he is known, Justin Martyr, reminds us that he, with many other Christians of his day, was ready to prove the reality of his faith by giving his life for it.

THE DIALOGUE WITH TRYPHO OF THE HOLY JUSTIN, PHILOSOPHER AND MARTYR.

I. How the Discussion with Trypho Began.

1. I was walking early one morning in the covered walk belonging to the Colonnade[1] when a man, with some companions, met me, and said, " Hullo, Philosopher!". And so saying he turned and walked along beside me, and his friends turned along with him. I in turn greeted him, and said, "Well?"

He answered: "I was taught in Argos by Corinthus the Socratic philosopher that people who wear the sort of dress which you are wearing should not be despised nor neglected, but they should be treated courteously and associated with in case some profit might result from the association, either to the other man or to me. For it is an advantage for both if either be helped. For this reason, whenever I see anyone in this dress, I approach him in a friendly way, and I was glad to accost you just now on the same principle, and these friends are accompanying me because they too expect to hear something useful from you."

" 'But who art thou, bravest of mortal men?' " was how I playfully replied to him.[2]

He told me straightforwardly both his name and his race. " I am called Trypho," he said; "I am a Hebrew,

[1]Probably at Ephesus.
[2]A quotation from Homer, the Shakespeare of men educated in ancient Greek culture.

from the circumcision, a refugee from the present war[1], and have spent a long time in Greece and in Corinth."

"Then," said I, "how could you possibly derive as much benefit from philosophy as you do from your own Lawgiver and from the prophets?"

"Why not? Do not the philosophers occupy all their discussion with the subject of God?" was his reply. "And their arguments on either side are about God's sole sovereignty and His providence. Or is not this the function of philosophy, to enquire about the divine?"

"Yes," I said, "this is what we think too. But the majority of philosophers are not interested in the subject of whether there is one God or many gods, and whether these gods take providential care of each one of us or not, on the grounds that this knowledge would achieve nothing towards gaining happiness. On the contrary, they try to persuade us that God does concern Himself about the whole universe and about the genera and species themselves, but not as far as about me and you and individual cases, because otherwise we would be praying to Him all night and all day. But it is not difficult to see where this argument finally leads them; for those who hold these opinions the result is irresponsibility and liberty both in word and in conduct, to do and to say whatever they like[2], because they have no fear of punishment and no hope of reward from God. What else could happen? They declare that the same events will recur eternally, and that you and I will live our lives again in just the same way without getting either better or worse. Another school

[1]This means the final Jewish revolt against the Romans, under Bar Cochba, which lasted from 132-135. But this *Dialogue* must have been written long after that period.
[2]An alternative (but not on the whole preferable) translation would run: "the result is irresponsibility and licence to utter these views and to follow those who hold them, and to do and say whatever they like".

presuppose that the soul is eternal and bodiless and that if they do anything wrong they think that they will not pay any penalty (for what is bodiless is incapable of suffering), and neither do they need anything more from God because the soul is immortal."

In reply he smiled urbanely and said, "Tell us what you think on these subjects and what belief you have about God and what your philosophy is."

2. "I will tell you what seems true to me at any rate," I said. "There is a genuine philosophy which is the best possession and one most honoured by God, and it alone leads us and commends us to God; and those who occupy their mind with philosophy are the really holy people. But most people have forgotten what philosophy is and the reason why it was sent down to men. Otherwise they would not be Platonists nor Stoics nor Peripatetics nor Speculatives, nor Pythagoreans, in spite of the existence of this unique science. I would like to explain how philosophy became divided into schools. It happened that those who first took it up and in consequence became famous were followed by the next generation who carried on no research about the truth but simply, impressed by their predecessors' perseverance and self-discipline and by the unusual quality of their utterances, thought that those doctrines were true which each man had learnt from his teacher; next they themselves, when they handed on to their juniors teachings such as these and others consistent with them, came to be called by that name by which the author of the system had been called. I too for my part was anxious like the others to meet one of these teachers, and I attached myself to a Stoic teacher. And when I had studied a long time with him, since no further information about God came to me (for he was not a believer in God himself and he did not think this doctrine essential), I rid myself of this teacher and

14

went to another, who called himself a Peripatetic and had a reputation as a shrewd man. And when he had put up with me for the first few days he decided then that the scale of his fees should be determined, so that our association should not be without profit. That was why I left him, thinking that he was no philosopher at all. But as my soul was still bursting to hear the peculiar and choice secret of philosophy, I moved on to a man who was very well spoken of, a Pythagorean, one who had devoted much thought to philosophy. And when I was anxious to become a hearer and disciple of his and entered into conversation with him, he said 'Well? Have you studied music and astronomy and geometry? Or do you think that you will perceive any of the things which assist towards happiness unless you have first learnt the studies which will detach the soul from tangible things and will render it able for intellectual things so that it can contemplate the Beautiful and the Truly Good?' When he had greatly praised these disciplines and declared them essential he sent me away, because I had acknowledged that I did not know them. I was upset therefore, as I well might be, because I was disappointed, and all the more because I conjectured that he did have some knowledge; but again when I calculated the time which I would be likely to spend on those disciplines, I could not bear to postpone everything for so long. In this state of resourcelessness it occurred to me to try the Platonists, for their fame was considerable. And consequently I constantly associated with a very learned man who had recently come to live in our town, and who was eminent among the Platonists, and I was making progress and improving more and more every day. Their conception of the bodiless things was attracting me greatly and the contemplation of the Ideas was exciting my mind and I thought that I had become wise in a short time, and in my stupidity I hoped to have a vision of God straight away; for this is the objective of Plato's philosophy.

3. Now when I was in this state of mind, intending to be filled with a great tranquillity and 'to shun the haunt of men'[1], I made a journey to a place which was not far from the sea. When I was near the spot where I intended to be quite alone, an old man whose appearance was not beneath notice and who gave the impression of possessing a gentle and respectable character, began almost shadowing me. I turned round to him, stopped, and inspected him keenly.

He said: 'Do you know me?'

'No,' I said.

'Then,' said he, 'why are you looking at me like that?'

'I am surprised,' I said, 'that you happen to be in the same place as I am, because I did not expect to see anybody else here.'

'I am looking after some of my slaves,' he said. 'They have run away from me, so I have made a personal visit to look for them, in case they turn up anywhere here. But what are you doing here?' he asked me.

'I am spending my time here for my own enjoyment,' I said. 'My discourse with myself meets no hindrance here, and places like these are conducive to the study of ideas.'

'So you study ideas, do you?' said he, 'and you never study deeds nor truth, nor try to be a man of action rather than an academic?'

'But,' said I, 'what better advantage could anyone achieve than to demonstrate the principle which governs all things and, having grasped it, from its vantage-point to survey the error of other people and their behaviour and to see how they do nothing right nor acceptable to God? Without philosophy and the right principle wisdom cannot be in anybody's possession. That is why everybody ought to study philosophy and regard this as the greatest and most

[1]Another Homeric quotation.

16

honourable activity and put everything else in second and
third place and think of things which are dependent upon
philosophy as proper and worth embracing, but activities
divorced from it and where it does not accompany those
who undertake them should be esteemed drudgery and
fit only for artisans.'

'So philosophy brings happiness?', he said in answer.

'Yes it does,' I said, 'and it alone.'

'Then what is philosophy,' he said, 'and what is the happiness attached to it? Explain, unless there is any reason
why you should not explain.'

'Philosophy,' I said, 'is the science of reality and the understanding of truth, and happiness is the reward of this science
and wisdom.'

'What do you think God is?' he said.

'That which eternally remains the Same in its existence and
its mode of existence, and is the cause of existence for all
other things, that is God.' This was my answer, and he was
glad when he heard me and then asked me this question:

'Is not science a common name given to diverse things?
For in all the crafts a man who is skilled in them is called
scientifically qualified; it is the same in military affairs, in
navigation and in medicine. But this does not hold of
divine and human matters. Is there a science which supplies
the knowledge of human affairs themselves and of divine
affairs, and the conviction of the latter's divinity and
righteousness?'

'Yes, there is,' I said.

'Well, then, is it the same thing to know man and God
as it is to know music and arithmetic and astronomy or
any of those subjects?'

'Far from it,' I said.

'Then you have given me a wrong answer,' he said.
'One sort of knowledge comes from study or experience,

the other gives science by vision. If I were to say to you that there is an animal living in India unlike all the other animals but with such and such an appearance, with many forms and many colours, you would not have previously known it or seen it, but you could not even give a description of it unless you had listened to somebody who had seen it.'

'No,' I said.

'Then,' said he, 'how can the philosophers think rightly about God or say anything true about him, as they have no science about him, they have never seen him nor heard him?'

'But sir,' I said, 'the divine is not visible to the physical eyes as are other living things, but can only be apprehended by the mind. This is what Plato says, and I agree with him.'

4. 'Is there then,' he said, 'in the mind a power sufficiently strong and appropriate, or perhaps it grasps reality by tangible means? Or will the mind of man never see God unless enriched by a holy spirit?'

'Well, Plato says,' I replied, 'that this very capacity is the eye of the mind and was given for this very purpose, to be able to see reality directly by its own power, that reality which is the cause of all intellectual things, which has no colour, no shape, no magnitude, nor any of the qualities visible to the eye, but somehow this very reality, says he, which is higher than all substance, which cannot be spoken about nor described, but is simply Beauty and Goodness, suddenly appears in souls whose nature is good, because of its kinship to them and the desire they have of seeing it.'

'Then what kinship,' said he, 'have we with God? Or is the soul divine and immortal and a part of that controlling mind already mentioned? And as it sees God so it is within our reach also to grasp the divine with our mind and thenceforward at once to be happy?'

'Certainly,' I said.

'And do all the souls of living creatures receive it in all cases,' he said, 'or is there one soul of men and another of a horse and an ass?'

'No, but the same souls are in all,' I answered.

'Then,' said he, 'horses and asses will see or have at some time seen God?'

'No,' I said, 'not even the majority of men, but only if a man were to live in justice, cleansing himself in righteousness and in every other virtue.'

'Therefore,' he said, 'he does not see God through kinship nor because he is mind, but because he is self-controlled and righteous.'

'Yes,' I said, 'and by having a capacity to perceive God.'

'What? So goats and sheep do wrong in some way?'

'No, they do not do anybody any wrong,' I said.

'Then,' said he, 'according to your argument these animals will also see God.'

'No, because the particular sort of body they have is an obstruction to them.'

'If those animals were to receive the power of speech,' he replied, 'you can be sure that they would disparage our body with much greater reason. But for the moment let us leave this argument as it is, and agree with what you say. But tell me this: does the soul have vision while it is in the body or when it is freed from the body?'

'While the soul is in a human form,' I said, 'it is possible for it to remain in it by means of the mind, but when it is released from the body and abides entirely by itself it much more achieves what it has been desiring all the time.'

'Does it remember this achievement when it is in a human being again?'

'I do not think so,' I said.

'What is the advantage for those souls who have had the vision, or what more has he who sees than he who does not see, if he does not remember this fact that he has had the vision?'

'I cannot answer that,' I replied.

'What happens to those souls who are judged unworthy of this vision?' he said.

'They are imprisoned in the bodies of various beasts, and this is their punishment.'

'They are aware, then, that this is the reason why they are in bodies of this sort, and that they have done something wrong?'

'I think not.'

'Apparently there is no advantage in their punishment, and I would not even say that they are being punished if they do not recognize the punishment.'

'No.'

'Then souls do not see God, nor do they change into other bodies. For if that were so they would know that they are being punished and they would be afraid of committing even the slightest wrong for the future. But that they can know that God exists and that righteousness and piety are good, with that I agree,' he said.

'You speak truly,' I said . . . .

[*Chapter* 5 *omitted*; *it establishes that souls are not immortal and that they are after this life reserved for punishment or reward.*]

6. 'I am not interested in Plato or Pythagoras,' he said, 'nor in fact in anyone who holds any sort of opinions like theirs. This is the true state of affairs, and you might as well learn it: The soul either is life or possesses life. If then it were life, it would communicate life to something else, not to itself. But nobody would deny that the soul lives. If it lives it lives not as being life but as sharing in life; what shares in something is distinct from that in which it shares. The soul shares in life since God wishes it to live. Similarly

20

then it will at some point no longer have a share when he does not wish it to live, for living is not its peculiar characteristic as it is God's; but just as a man does not exist indefinitely and his body does not permanently co-exist with his soul, but when this combination must be dissolved the soul deserts the body and the man exists no longer, so when the soul must no longer exist the life-giving spirit deserts it and it is a soul no longer but of its own accord it goes back again to the place from where it was taken.'

7. 'What teacher could anyone employ then,' I said, 'or how could anyone get any assistance, if the truth is not in these philosophers?'

'There were men a very long time ago more ancient than these who are reputed to be philosophers, blessed and righteous and dear to God. They spoke by a divine spirit and they oracularly predicted future events which are now taking place. They are called prophets. They alone saw the truth and declared it to men; they did not suffer from timidity nor embarrassment nor were they influenced by ambition, but they spoke only those things which they had heard and seen when they were filled with a holy Spirit. Their writings remain to this day and it is possible for anyone who studies them to gain much enlightenment about first principles and the final consummation and everything which a philosopher ought to know, if a man will but believe them. They have not set out their accounts with formal argument, but as witnesses of the truth worthy of belief, as if they were above all formal argument. Past events and events now taking place compel us to agree with what was spoken by them. Furthermore they deserved to be believed because of the miracles which they performed, since they were glorifying God the Creator and Father of the universe and they were announcing the Christ coming from him, his Son. This the false prophets who were filled with the deceitful and filthy spirit never did nor now do, but they dare to operate various miracles in order to impress men and they glorify the spirits and demons of deceit[1]. You should pray above all that the gates of light may be opened to you, for these things are not intelligible and comprehensible to everybody unless God and his Christ give understanding to a man.'

8. This man told me these facts, and many others, which there is not time now to relate, and then departed, enjoining me to investigate them, and I never saw him again. Immediately a fire was lit in my soul, and a desire for the prophets seized me and for those men who are friends of Christ; as I turned over his words in my mind I found this the only reliable and profitable philosophy. In fact this is the way and these the means whereby I am a philosopher. I would like everybody to conceive a determination equal with mine not to abandon the doctrines of the Saviour. For they include among them a certain menace, and they are sufficient to discourage those who are turning away from the right road, and also the most delightful refreshment exists for those who practise them. If therefore you are concerned about yourself and are anxious to gain salvation, and trust in God, believing him not to be irrelevant to this matter[2], it is possible for you to know God's Christ, to become initiated and to be happy."

When I had said this, my dear friend[3], Trypho's companions laughed, but he smiled and said:

"I accept the rest of your opinions and am impressed with your enthusiasm for religion. But it would be better for you to follow the philosophical system of Plato or of any

[1] Tim. 4:1.
[2] Or, "as you are not unacquainted with the subject"; but I think not.
[3] The book, as becomes evident in cap.141, is dedicated to a Marcus Pompeius, otherwise unknown.

22

other philosopher, practising perseverance and self-discipline and temperance, than to be deceived by false words and follow worthless men. For if you were to remain in your original course of philosophy and live irreproachably, the hope of a better destiny would be retained; but what salvation is available for somebody who trusts in man? If you wish to be persuaded by me (for I have already regarded you as a friend), first undergo circumcision, then in accordance with the law observe the sabbath and the major and minor feasts of God, and, in short, do all the things that are written in the law, and then perhaps one day there will be mercy for you from God. If the Christ has been born and exists somewhere, he is incognito and does not even recognize himself, and has no power, until Elijah comes and anoints him and makes him manifest to all. You have received a futile rumour, and have invented some sort of Christ for yourselves, and for his sake you are now unreflectingly going into perdition."

9. "My dear man," I said, "may you receive pardon and be forgiven. You do not know what you are saying but you are influenced by your teachers and you pontificate and say whatever accords with your mood. If you are ready you can hear an account of how we are not deceived and will not cease preaching this Christ even though slanders are hurled against us by human agency, even though the fiercest tyrant would compel us to recant. For I will show you, if you pay attention, we have not put our trust in empty legends nor in arguments incapable of proof, but in a religion full of a divine spirit and bursting with power and blossoming with grace." At this his companions again burst into laughter and made an unseemly uproar. So I got to my feet and prepared to go off. But he took hold of my coat and said that he would not let me go until I had done what I promised. "Well," said I, "your companions must not

make a disturbance nor behave in this rude way. But if they choose to they can listen quietly, or if more important business prevents them let them go away. I suggest that we should retire somewhere and, having had a rest, finish our argument." Trypho agreed to follow this plan and we turned off and went into the space in the middle of the Colonnade, but two of his companions, joking and laughing at our earnestness, went off. When we reached that place where there are stone seats on each side, Trypho's companions sat down on one of them and one of the men started a conversation about the war in Judaea, and they began talking among themselves.

II. The Old Testament Law was Destined to be Superseded by another Covenant.

10. When they had finished I began speaking to them again thus:

"My friends, is the only fault which you have to find with us that we do not live according to the law, and are not circumcised in our flesh like your forefathers and do not keep the sabbath as you do? Or do imputations against our life and behaviour circulate among you? What I mean is, do you also believe about us that we are allegedly cannibals and that after a banquet we extinguish the lights and have orgies of unnatural intercourse; or do you only condemn in us the fact that we are attached to doctrines of the sort which you have described and that we believe in a creed which is, as you think, a false one?"

"This last point is what amazes us," said Trypho, "but as for the popular assertions, they are not worth believing, because they are alien from human nature. Further, the

exhortations contained in what is called the gospel I understand to be so extraordinary and demanding that I suspect
that nobody can keep them, for I have taken the trouble to
look into them. But we are perplexed most of all that you
who profess to be pious and think that you excel others do
not abandon their practices in any point nor alter your
manner of life from that of the Gentiles, in as far as you do
not observe the festivals nor the sabbaths nor keep up circumcision. Another point, you set your hopes on a crucified
man and yet you hope to gain some reward from God,
without obeying his commandments. Or have you not
read that *that soul will be destroyed from its race which will not
be circumcised on the eighth day*?[1] The same commandment
is given about the foreigner and the foreign born slaves.
This covenant you directly despise and the later ones, and
you try to convert us as if you knew God, though you
keep none of the customs which the proselytes do. If
therefore you have any defence to make to this and can show
in any way that you have a ground of hope, even though
you do not keep the law, this is what we would be particularly glad to hear, and we might examine the other
subjects in the same way."

11. At that I answered him, "Trypho, there will never
be any other God, nor was there from eternity, except the
creator and orderer of this universe. We do not imagine
that you have one God and we another, but that same God
who *brought out* your fathers from the land of Egypt *with
a strong hand and a high arm*[2]. We have not hoped in any
other, for none exists, but on this same one as you do, the
God of Abraham and Isaac and Jacob. But we have not
hoped in him through Moses nor through the law, otherwise
we should be doing just as you do. In fact, Trypho, I have

[1]Gen. 17:14.
[2]Deut. 5:15 or Ps. 135 (136):12.

read that there was to be a final law and a covenant more authoritative than any other, which all men must now observe who lay claim to God's inheritance. For the law of Horeb is now antiquated and was for you alone, but this one is for all without discrimination. A law which is given in contrast to another cancels the previous one and similarly a covenant which takes place later renders the former one void. Christ has been given to us as an everlasting and final law, and this covenant is reliable after which there is neither law nor ordinance nor commandment" . . .[1].

[*There follow quotations from Isa.* 51:4,5; *Jer.* 38 (31), 31,32.]

"If therefore God declared that a new covenant was destined to be established and that this one was to be for a light to the Gentiles, we see and we are convinced that through the name of this crucified Jesus Christ men leave the idols and other wickedness and approach God and endure as far as death in order to maintain their profession and their worship. And it is open to all to understand from their actions and from the power that accompanies them that this is the new law and the new covenant and the *obedience* of men coming from *all peoples*[2] and waiting upon God's rewards. We are the true spiritual race of Israel and of Judah and of Jacob and Isaac and Abraham, who was witnessed to by God *in uncircumcision*, through faith, and *blessed* and called the *father of many nations*[3], for we have been brought near to God through this crucified Christ, as will be demonstrated as our arguments develop."

19. And Trypho said: "This is enough to bewilder anyone, that you endure any sort of ill-treatment, and yet you do not observe all the other ordinances about which we are having this discussion."

[1]Cap. 11:3 is omitted.
[2]Gen. 49:10.
[3]Gen. 17:5; 24:1,12; cf. Rom. 4:10.

26

(Justin) "Circumcision is not necessary for everybody, but only for you, so that you may, as I have already said, experience the sufferings which you now justly experience. We regard that cistern-baptism of yours as futile; it has nothing to do with that baptism which is the baptism of life. This is why God cried aloud, *You have deserted him, the living fountain, and you have dug for yourselves broken cisterns which will not be able to hold water*[1]. You who have physical circumcision need our circumcision, but we, having our own, do not need yours. If circumcision had been necessary, as you believe, God would not have created Adam uncircumcised, nor would he have *looked upon the gifts of Abel* who was offering sacrifices in physical uncircumcision, nor would *Enoch*, in a state of uncircumcision, have *pleased* him, *and he was not found, because God translated him*[2]. Lot *was saved from Sodom*[3] when uncircumcised, escorted by angels sent from the Lord. Noah, the originator of a new race, *went with his sons into the ark*[4] uncircumcised. *Melchizedek, priest of the Most High*, was uncircumcised. To him Abraham, who was the first to receive physical circumcision, *gave tithes* as offerings, and Melchizedek *blessed* him[5]; it was according to his order that God recorded through David that he would set up the everlasing priest[6]. This circumcision was necessary for you alone, so that the people *might not be a people*[7] and the race no race, as Hosea, one of the minor prophets, says. Further, all these righteous men just named never observed the sabbath, and yet pleased God, and after them Abraham and all his sons as far down as Moses, during whose time your

[1]Jer. 2:13.
[2]Gen. 4:4; 5:24.
[3]Gen. 19:17-20.
[4]Gen. 7:13.
[5]Gen. 14:18-20.
[6]Ps. 109 (110):4.
[7]Hos. 1:9.

27

race proved unrighteous and unthankful to God when they made the calf in the wilderness. This was why God, adapting the practice to this people, ordained also that they should offer sacrifices as if in his name, to prevent you indulging in idolatry; but you did not even avoid this, but you even sacrificed your children to demons. And he commanded you to keep the sabbath so that you should preserve a memory of God. The Word, moreover, indicates this when he says, *So that you should know that I am your God who redeemed you*[1].

20. Again, he enjoined you to refrain from certain kinds of food, in order that when you eat and drink you should have God before your eyes, because you are unstable and easily inclined to revolt from the knowledge of him.

[Here follows a quotation of *Deut*. 32:15.]

It is recorded by the hand of Moses in the book of Genesis that it was permitted by Noah, a righteous man, to eat every living thing, except *meat with the blood in it*, that is, a carcase."[2]

And as Trypho was trying to say "*As green herbs*"[3], I forestalled him and said "Could you not interpret the phrase '*as green herbs*' as the statement by God that as God made herbs for food for man, so he gave the animals for meat to eat? But since we do not eat some sorts of herbs, so you allege that a distinction (of meats) was then being imposed on Noah. Your interpretation is unconvincing. First because I could say that every herb is in fact good and can be eaten, and I could carry conviction, but I will not spend time on that argument. Secondly, even if we do distinguish herbs from food, and do not eat all herbs, we do not refrain

[1]Exod. 20: 12,20.
[2]Gen. 9:3,4.
[3]Trypho was going to argue that as we distinguish between edible and inedible herbs, so God meant to distinguish between one class of legitimate and another of illegitimate sorts of meat.

because they are common and unclean, but either because they are sour or poisonous or prickly. But we do search for and partake of all those that are sweet and nourishing and the best, gathered either by the sea or on land. Thus it was that God commanded you through Moses to refrain from everything filthy and wrong and lawless, because in spite of your eating manna in the desert and seeing all the wonderful events which happened to you from God, you made the golden calf and worshipped it. So the righteous one continually cries out, *Foolish sons, there is no faith in you.*"[1]

III. The Two Comings of Christ.

[*Caps. 12-18 and 21-30(2) are occupied with a demonstration that all Jewish institutions and ceremonies were intended to be temporary and to point towards their spiritual counterparts in Christianity, and that the Jews wilfully misunderstood them.*]
(*Justin is speaking*)

30(3) "We constantly pray God through Jesus Christ that we may be preserved from the demons, who are alien to the cult of God, and whom we used to worship, so that after turning to God through him we may be blameless. For we call him a helper and a redeemer before the power of whose name even the demons tremble, and they are daily exorcized and submit in the name of Jesus Christ who was crucified under Pontius Pilate who was governor of Judaea, so that from this fact it is clear to all that his Father gave him great enough authority for the demons to submit to his name and to the divine policy manifested in the suffering which he endured.

31. Now if so much authority is shown to have accompanied and still to be accompanying the divine policy

[1]Jer. 4:22.

shown in his suffering, how great will be the authority attached to his glorious Coming when it takes place! For he will come as the Son of Man seated on clouds, as Daniel recorded, with angels accompanying him." [*There follows a quotation from Dan. 7:9-28.*]

32. And when I ceased, Trypho said, "My dear man, these passages and others like them compel us to look for some glorious and great figure receiving the everlasting kingdom as Son of Man from the Ancient of Days. But this man of yours who was called Christ was of humble origin and obscure, so much so that he even incurred the very last curse of God, for he was crucified."

I replied to him: "My argument would appear silly and incompetent, my friends, if I had not, as I have already recounted, expounded from the Scriptures that his *form* was said to be inglorious and his *race indescribable*, and that the *rich should be put to death for his death* and that *we were healed by his stripe* and that he was to be *led away as a sheep*[1], and that two Comings of his were to take place, one in which *he was pierced* by you, the other in which *you shall recognize him whom you have pierced*, and *all your tribes shall mourn, tribe by tribe, the women separately and the men separately*[2]. But as it is I have been producing proof texts throughout all our discussion from the prophetic Scriptures which are regarded as holy by you, in the hope that somebody among you might be found among that *remnant* which is preserved by the grace of the *Lord of Hosts*[3] for everlasting salvation. But now, so that the subject under discussion should become clearer to you, I will relate to you some other passages spoken through the blessed David, from which you will perceive that the Christ is called Lord by the holy prophetic Spirit

[1] Isa. 53:2,3,5,7-9.
[2] Zech. 12:10,12; Rev. 1:7.
[3] Isa. 1:9.

and that the Father who is *Lord* of all has brought him up from the earth and *seated* him *on his right hand, until he should put his enemies as a footstool under his feet*[1]. This has been the state of affairs since our Lord Jesus Christ was taken up into heaven after he had been raised from the dead. The times are being fulfilled, and he who is destined to speak blasphemous and daring words against the Most High is even now at the doors, he whom Daniel declares to be destined to hold dominion for *a time and times and half a time*[2].

[There follow expositions of Dan. 7:25, 2 Thess. 2:3 and Jer. 4.22 conflated with Isa. 29:14 and Ps. 109 (110) 1-7] . . .[3].

35.7. From these passages, as I have said, we take Jesus to have been a forecaster of events destined to happen after him, and from many other experiences which he foretold as about to happen to those who believed in him and confessed him as Christ. He also foretold as destined to happen all the sufferings which we are enduring, when betrayed to execution by our own slaves, so that neither his speech nor his actions can appear open to blame. That is why we pray both for you and for all other men who display hostility to us, that you may repent with us and many not slander him who is shown to be entirely irreproachable and innocent both by his actions and by the miracles which are even now taking place in his name, and by the principles of his teaching and by the prophecies which were predicted about him, Christ Jesus. May you on the contrary believe in him and be saved at his glorious Coming Again when it takes place, and not be condemned to the fire by him."

[The question has been raised in cap. 45, who are to share in the resurrection from the dead? Are the Jews to do so?]

(Trypho is speaking)

[1]Ps 109 (110):1.
[2]Dan. 7:25.
[3]Cap. 33:1-35:6 omitted.

46. He asked me: "If there are some people who want to follow a course of life observing the ordinances imposed by Moses and also believe in this crucified Jesus, recognizing that he is the Christ of God and that to him is granted authority to judge every single person, and his is the everlasting kingdom, can such people be saved too?"

I said in reply, "Let us consider this point, whether it is possible to observe now all the ordinances imposed by Moses."

He answered: "No. We recognize that, as you have said, it is not possible to slay the Passover lamb elsewhere than in Jerusalem, nor for those who are commanded to do so to sacrifice goats at the Day of Atonement, nor in fact any of the other sacrifices." I said, "Which ones then is it possible to observe? I ask you to tell me yourself. For you will be convinced that a man can certainly be saved who does not observe or do the everlasting ordinances." He answered, "I would say, to keep the sabbath and to be circumcised and to keep the monthly feasts and to observe ritual washing after touching any of the things forbidden by Moses or after having sexual intercourse."

I said, "There were Abraham and Isaac and Jacob and Noah and Job, and all the other similarly righteous people who lived before them or after them, I mean Sarah the wife of Abraham and Rebecca the wife of Isaac and Rachel the wife of Jacob, and Leah, and all the other women of this sort until the mother of *Moses, the faithful servant*[1]. They observed none of these ordinances. Do you think they will be saved?"

Trypho answered: "Were not Abraham and the people later than he circumcised?"

I replied, "I believe that Abraham and those who came after him were circumcised. But I told the reason why

[1]Num. 12:7.

circumcision was given to them on many occasions during my earlier arguments, and unless the discussion is annoying you, let us examine the point again. You realize that until Moses absolutely no righteous person observed a single one of the ordinances which we have been discussing and received no command to observe them, except that circumcision took its starting-point in Abraham."

He said, "We realize this, and we admit that they are saved."

I replied, "You should know that it was because of the hardness of heart of your people that God enjoined all these ordinances on you through Moses, so that as you frequently practised many of them you should always have God before your eyes and initiate no wrongdoing nor impiety. He enjoined you to wear the scarlet fringe[1] so that thereby no forgetfulness of God should overtake you; and he ordered you to clasp round you a phylactery[2] containing very thin parchments on which are written some letters, which we too certainly consider holy, and thereby he challenged you perpetually to preserve the memory of God, and at the same time to have a sense of sin in your hearts. So you have many reminders of piety, but even so you were not persuaded to avoid idolatry, but in the time of Elijah when he calculated the number of men *who had not bowed the knee to Baal* he said that they were seven thousand[3], and in Isaiah he convicts you of even offering your *children as a sacrifice to idols*[4]. But we in order to avoid sacrificing to the things to whom we used to sacrifice, endure the very worst punishments and when we are put to death we rejoice, believing that God will raise us up through his Christ and render us no longer subject to

[1]So, by adopting an emendation; see Num. 15:37-41.
[2]They were contained in very small boxes; on the parchment were written the texts Exod. 13:1-10,11-16; Deut. 6:4-9; 11:13-21.
[3]1 Kings 19:18.
[4]Isa. 57:5.

33

corruption and suffering and death. And we know that the
ordinances imposed because of your people's hardness of heart
do not at all conduce to right conduct and right worship."

IV. The Pre-Existence and Divine Nature of Christ.

*[Chapters 49 and 50 argue that John the Baptist was endowed
with the spirit of Elijah to anoint the Christ before the Day of
Judgment.]*

(Justin is speaking)

54. "Now this account by Moses of the prophecy of the
patriarch Jacob, namely, *He shall wash his garment in wine
and his cloak in the blood of the grape*[1], was revealing that he
should wash those who believed in him in his blood. For
by *his garment* the Holy Spirit meant those who received
remission of sins through him, among whom he is always
present in power and will be visibly present at his Second
Coming. In using the phrase *the blood of the grape* the Spirit
indicated by artifice that though Christ has blood it is not
from the seed of men but from the power of God. For just
as it is not man who has produced the blood of the grape,
but God, so he predicted that the blood of Christ was not
to be of human stock but of the power of God. My friends,
this very prophecy which I have mentioned shows that Christ
is not a man descended from men, begotten according to the
common way of men."

55. Then Trypho interposed: "We shall remember this
exposition of yours also, if you solve this problem by other
proof-texts as well. But now return to your argument
and demonstrate to us that another God in addition to the
Creator of the world is declared by the Prophetic Spirit to
exist. You must be careful to rule out *the sun and the moon*

[1]Gen. 49:11.

which, it is written, *God agreed that the Gentiles should worship as gods*[1]. And the prophets often use this word 'god' in an artificial sense and say that *your God is the God of gods and the Lord of lords*[2], and they often add the epithets 'great and mighty and terrible'. They do not say this as though there really were gods, but because the Word is teaching us that the real God, the Creator of the universe, is alone Lord of all who are thought to be gods and lords. For in order that the Holy Spirit should confirm this he said through holy David, *the gods of the Gentiles*, the so-called gods, *are the images of demons* but not gods. And he invokes a curse on *those who make them*[3] and worship them."

I replied: "I had no intention, Trypho, of bringing forward these proof-texts, by which I understand that people who worship these idols and ones like them are condemned, but proof-texts which nobody will be able to refute. They will seem strange to you, although they are read by you daily, and you can understand from this that because of your own wickedness God has hidden from you the capacity to perceive the wisdom which is in his words, except for some, in whose case according to the grace of his great compassion, as Isaiah says, *he left a seed*[4] for salvation, that your entire race should not, like Sodom and Gomorrah, perish. Pay attention therefore to the texts which I am going to cite from the holy Scriptures; they scarcely need to be expounded but only to be heard.

56. Moses is the first witness, informing us of the God who appeared to Abraham by the oak of Mamre along with the two angels who were sent for judgment on the men of Sodom by another being, him who continually lives in the

[1]Deut. 4:19; 10:17.
[2]Deut. 10:17.
[3]Ps. 113:16 (115:8).
[4]Isa. 1:9.

region beyond the heavens and is seen by nobody and associates only with himself, whom we recognize as the Creator and Father of the universe." [*Here follows a quotation of Gen.* 18:1-3.] And ceasing to quote any further I asked them if they recognized the passage.

They said that they recognized it, but that the passages quoted were irrelevant to prove that another God or Lord beside the Creator of the universe exists or was spoken of by the Holy Spirit. I replied, "I will try to convince you of what I say, because you know these passages, that there is, and there is mentioned, another God and Lord below the Creator of the universe, who is also called a messenger (angel) because he delivers as a message to men whatever the Creator of the universe wants him to deliver, the Creator above whom there is no other God." And repeating my previous words I asked Trypho, "Do you think that God was seen under the oak at Mamre by Abraham, as the story relates?"

He said, "Yes."

"And," said I, "he was one of those three whom the holy prophetic Spirit describes as men seen by Abraham?"

He said, "No. But God had been seen by him before the appearance of these three. Then these three, whom the story calls men, were angels, two of them sent for the destruction of Sodom, and one sent to bring the good news to Sarah that she was to have a son. This was his commission and when he had completed it he departed."

"Then," said I, "how is it that one of the three who was in the tent, who was also the one that said '*In due season I will return to you and Sarah shall have a son*'[1], appears to have returned when Sarah did have a son, and the prophetic word there indicates that he was God? Listen to what was explicitly said by Moses: [*Here follows a quotation of Gen.* 21: [1]Gen. 18:14.

36

9-12.] Notice now that he who then said under the oak that he would return (for he knew beforehand that it would be necessary to give Abraham advice about the demands Sarah would make on him) did return, as it is written, and is God, as the words indicate which run thus: *God said to Abraham; let it not be difficult in your sight concerning the child and concerning the slavegirl[1]*". This was the question asked. Trypho said, "Yes. By this argument you have not proved that there is another God as well as this one seen by Abraham, who was seen also by other patriarchs and prophets, but you have shown that we were not correct in our opinion that the three figures who were in the tent with Abraham were simply angels"[2] ... I said in reply, "Returning to the Scriptures, I will try to convince you that this figure who is mentioned and described as seen by Abraham and Isaac and Moses is another God than the God who is Creator of the universe, other in number, I mean, not in will, for I do not assert that he ever did anything except what the Creator of the world, above whom there is no other God, intended both to do and to say."

And Trypho: "Prove now that he exists, so that we may agree on this point. We do not suppose that you assert that he says or did or uttered anything apart from the will of the Creator of the universe."

I said, "The passage already quoted by me will demonstrate this to you". [*Here Justin quotes Gen. 19:23-25.*]

The fourth companion who had remained behind with Trypho said: "We are compelled to admit that one of the two angels who came down to Sodom whom Moses' story called Lord is different from God himself who was seen by Moses."[3]

[1] Gen. 21:12.
[2] Paragraph 10 is omitted.
[3] 56:14-22 is omitted.

[*The rest of the chapter labours to prove that the three figures who appeared to Abraham in the incidents already discussed were two angels accompanying the second or inferior God and Lord to whom, Justin maintains, the Old Testament witnesses.*]

57. While I was silent Trypho said: "It is clear that Scripture compels us to acknowledge this. But you would agree that it is right to be perplexed about the passage which says that (the angel) *ate* the things prepared by Abraham and *put before him.*"[1] I answered: "It is written that they ate. I suppose we are to assume that the three are said to have eaten, not just the two, who were really angels and, it is evident to us, were fed in the heavens, even though not fed on the kind of food which we men eat (for the Scripture says this about the manna, with which your fathers were fed in the wilderness, *they ate angels' food*)[2]. So I would conjecture that the account which says that they ate would mean much what we would if we said about fire that it devoured everything, but we are not at all to interpret the passage as if they ate chewing with teeth and jaws. Consequently we would not be perplexed about any point in this passage if we have even the least experience of using figurative language."

Trypho: "It is possible that the problem raised by the method of eating by which according to Scripture they consumed and ate the food prepared by Abraham can be solved. So come now and give us the reason why this God who was seen by Abraham, and who was the servant of the God Creator of the universe, came to be born of a virgin and to be a man with the same consciousness as all men, as you have already said"[3] . . .

[1]Gen. 18:8.
[2]Ps. 77(78): 25.
[3]57:4,58,59,60 is omitted.

(*Justin speaking*)

61. "My friends," I said, "I will give you another testimony from the Scriptures that God produced a Beginning before all created things, a rational power coming from himself, which is also called by the Holy Spirit the glory of the Lord[1], who sometimes calls himself Son, and sometimes Angel, and sometimes God, and sometimes Lord and Word and sometimes *Captain of the Host*[2], when he appeared in the form of a man to Joshua of Nun. All his names are derived from the fact that he serves the Father's purpose and that he was begotten from the Father by his will. Do we not indeed see a similar phenomenon taking place in our own experience? When we utter any word, we originate this word but do not produce it by means of division, as if the reason (word) in us were thereby reduced. But the process is like what we see when one fire is kindled from another; the fire from which the kindling came is not reduced but remains the same and the fire which was kindled from it also appears to be lighting on its own without reducing that from which it was kindled. The account of wisdom will supply me with a testimony here, wisdom which is this same God begotten by the Father of the universe, who exists also as Word and Wisdom and Power and Glory of its begetter."

[*Here follows a quotation of Prov.* 8:21-36.]

62. "The Word of God, my friends, said this very same thing through Moses informing us that he whom he had indicated was by the same conception called God in the passage describing the creation of man.

[*Here follows a quotation of Gen.* 1:26-28.]

Now you may by altering the words just quoted take the same view as your teachers, either that, when God said

[1] Exod. 16:7.
[2] Josh. 5:14.

Let us make[1], he was talking to himself, just as we, when we are going to make something, often say to ourselves, 'Let us make'; or that God said *Let us make* to the elements, that is to the earth and to the other ingredients of which we know man to have been composed. But to prevent you thinking this I will again repeat the words said by Moses himself, from which we can know indisputably that he conversed with another being, different in number and rational. These are the words: *And God said, Behold Adam has become as one of us to know good and evil*[2]. Surely when he said *As one of us*, he indicated a number of people present together, and at least two. For I would not agree that the view held by a sect among you is true, either that the teachers of this sect can demonstrate that he was speaking to angels or that the human body was the creation of angels. But this being, really produced by the Father, co-existed with the Father before all created things, and the Father was conversing with him, as the Word declared through Solomon, to the effect that this same being was a Beginning before all created things and was produced as an offspring by God which is called Wisdom by Solomon, and just the same thing was declared by the revelation which took place to Joshua son of Nun." [*A quotation of Josh.5:13-6:2 follows.*]

[*Cap.64 tries to establish from Pss. 99 and 72 that the same being is witnessed to in the O.T., and Cap. 65 instances Isa. 42: 5-13 for the same purpose.*]

V. The Earthly Life of Jesus.

66. I again took up the argument at the point where originally I had stopped in my demonstration that he was

[1]Gen. 1:26.
[2]Gen. 3:22.

born from a Virgin and that a prophecy had been made through Isaiah that he would be born through a Virgin.

[*Here follow citations of Isa. 7:10-17 and 8:4.*]

And I added, "It is clear to everybody that no one of the physical descendants of Abraham was ever born of a virgin or is recorded as so born except this our Christ."

67. Trypho answered, "The passage does not say, *Behold, the virgin shall conceive in the womb and shall bring forth a son*[1], but *Behold, the young woman shall conceive in the womb and shall bring forth a son*, and so on, as you said. The whole prophecy is to be applied to Hezekiah, and it is demonstrable that the events happened to Hezekiah according to the prophecy. And in the legends of those who are called the Greeks it is related that Perseus was born of Danae while she was a virgin after he who is called Zeus among them had flowed into her in the form of a stream of gold. You ought to be ashamed of retailing the same tales as the Greeks, and should rather say that this Jesus was born as a human being from human beings, and, if you are demonstrating from the Scriptures that he is the Christ, you should say that he earned the appointment as Christ by his perfect behaviour in obedience to the law, but you should not dare to tell fairy stories, in case you are convicted of the same futility as that of the Greeks."

I replied to this, "Trypho, I want to convince you and everybody I can that even if you laugh at me or even indulge in worse mockery you will not move me from my intended line of argument, but I will continue to produce proofs of my assertion with testimony from the Scriptures from the very arguments which you think you are bringing forward to refute me. You are not acting either consistently or honestly when you try to demolish a position about which

[1]Isa. 7:14.

41

we have already come to agreement, that some of the commandments were imposed through Moses owing to the hardness of your nation's heart. For you said that it was owing to his observance of the law that he was chosen Christ and became Christ, assuming that he has been demonstrated to be Christ."

Trypho said: "Yes, because you have conceded to us that he was circumcised and he observed all the other legal ordinances imposed through Moses."

I answered: "I conceded it and I do concede it, but I do not admit that he endured all this discipline on the grounds that he was justified by it, but because he was carrying out the divine policy which his Father and the Creator of the universe and Lord and God willed. I also admit that he endured death by crucifixion and all the terrible sufferings which the men of your nation inflicted on him[1]" . . .

69. I added, "You can be sure, Trypho, that the very stories which he who is called the devil deceitfully caused to be told among the Greeks, just as he operated through the wise men of Egypt and the false prophets in the time of Elijah, have confirmed my understanding and faith in the Scriptures. For when they say that Dionysus was born as the son of Zeus as a result of his intercourse with Semele, and when they relate that this Dionysus was the inventor of the vine, and that he was torn in pieces and died and rose again and went up to heaven, and when they introduce an ass into his mysteries, can I not recognize that he has imitated the prophecy spoken beforehand by the patriarch Jacob and recorded by Moses[2]? And when they describe Hercules as strong and as journeying through the whole earth and that he was born to Zeus of Alcmena and that he died and went into heaven, do I not recognize an imitation of the passage

[1]67:7-11 and 68 are omitted.
[2]Gen. 49:11,12.

of Scripture spoken about Christ, *He is strong as a giant to run his course?*[1] And when he introduces Asclepius raising the dead and curing other human ills am I not to say that he is imitating the prophecies made about Christ on this subject in this instance too? But since I have not yet repeated to you a passage of this sort which indicates that Christ will perform these acts, I will have to remind you of one, from which it will be possible to understand how the Word foretold even to those who were destitute of the knowledge of God, I mean the Gentiles, who *though they had eyes did not see and though they had intelligence could not understand, who worship things composed of wood*[2], that they would abandon these things and hope in this Christ.

[*A quotation from Isa. 35:1-7 follows.*]

This Christ sprang up as a fountain of living water in the land destitute of the knowledge of God, the land of the Gentiles; he also was manifested to your race and healed those who were from birth physically maimed and deaf and lame, causing one to leap and another to hear and a third to see at his word. And he raised the dead and gave them life and by his actions challenged the men of that time to recognize him. Those who saw these events taking place alleged that it was a magical illusion, and indeed they dared to call him a sorcerer and a deceiver of the people. But he used to perform these acts in order to persuade those who were likely to believe in him that even if anybody who had some bodily defect turned out to be an observer of the doctrines delivered by him he would raise him up whole at his Second Coming after he had rendered him immortal and immune from corruption or sorrow.

70. When those who hand on the mysteries of Mithras relate that he was born from a rock and call the place a cave

[1] Ps. 18(19):6.
[2] Ps. 113:12-16 (115:4-8); Isa.6:10.

43

where they initiate into their traditions those who believe in him, can I not perceive that in this case they are imitating the saying of Daniel that *A stone was cut without hands from a great mountain*, and a similar passage in Isaiah, the whole of whose utterances they attempted to imitate[1]? For they have arranged that words urging right conduct should be spoken in their rites.

[*There follows a quotation from Isa. 33:13-19.*]

It is clear that in this prophecy mention is made of the bread which our Christ taught us to make in remembrance of his becoming incarnate[2] for the sake of those who believe in him, for whose sake he even became vulnerable to suffering, and of the cup, which he taught us to make in the eucharist in remembrance of his blood[3]. And this same prophecy indicates that we shall see him as a King with glory. And these passages of the prophecy cry aloud that that people which was foreknown to be destined to believe in him was foreknown to be destined to practise the fear of the Lord. And that those who imagine that they know the text of the Scriptures, and who hear the prophecies read, have no understanding the same Scriptures likewise proclaim. So, Trypho, whenever I hear that Perseus was begotten of a virgin, I realize that the deceitful serpent is imitating in this detail too.

71. But I do not assent to your teachers when they refuse to accept as a proper translation that which was made by the Seventy Elders in the reign of Ptolemy who was King of Egypt, but try to produce their own translations. I would like you to realize that they have entirely removed many passages from the translation of the elders under Ptolemy, in which this same crucified man is indicated, declared directly

[1]Dan. 2:34; cf. Isa. 33:16.
[2]Or "of his becoming incorporate" (i.e. in the eucharist).
[3]1 Cor. 11:23-25.

to be God and man and crucified and dying[1]. I am not
bringing these texts into evidence, because I understand that
everybody of your race rejects them, but I am here to conduct
the discussion from the texts which are still acknowledged
by you. Consequently you are acquainted with such of the
texts as I have brought to your notice, except that you
attack the verse *Behold, the virgin shall conceive in the womb*[2],
and allege that it runs *Behold the young woman shall conceive
in the womb*. And I promised to demonstrate formally that
the prophecy does not apply to Hezekiah, as you have been
taught, but to this Christ of mine. And indeed I will do
so."

Trypho said, "We request first that you will tell us some
of the passages which you allege to have been entirely
omitted."

[*Caps.72-77 give these quotations; which consist either of
purely Christian additions to the LXX or of passages which
are in Hebrew but have no particular reference to Christ.*]
(*Justin is speaking*)

78. "Consequently this King Herod enquired of the
elders of your people when the wise men from Arabia came
and told him that from a star which appeared in heaven they
knew that a king had been born in your country and that We
have come to worship him[3]. The elders said, In Bethlehem,

[1] Justin is referring to the Septuagint Greek translation of the Old
Testament, made in stages over a long period, beginning perhaps
about 270 B.C. The story of it having been made by seventy Jewish
translators sent for by Ptolemy I, King of Egypt, is largely legendary,
but there is no doubt that Alexandria is the place where this translation was begun. Justin's accusation that those passages which the
Septuagint contains but which are absent from the Hebrew Scriptures
were deliberately suppressed by the Jews is childish and absurd. The
Jews of his day were entirely justified in preferring the text of the
Hebrew.
[2] Isa. 7:14.
[3] The N.T. passages referred to in this section are Matt. 2:5 sq. and
1:18-20.

because this is written in the prophet: *And thou, Bethlehem, the country of Judah, art not least among the leaders of Judah, for out of thee shall come a leader, who shall shepherd my people*[1]. The wise men from Arabia came to Bethlehem and worshipped the child and offered to him gifts, gold and frankincense and myrrh. Then by revelation, after they had worshipped the child in Bethlehem, they were commanded not to go back again to Herod. And Joseph who was betrothed to Mary, though he had previously intended to abandon Mary who was betrothed to him, because he thought that she was pregnant as a result of intercourse with a man, that is as a result of fornication, was commanded by a vision not to abandon his wife, for the angel who appeared to him said to him, 'What she has in her womb is from the Holy Spirit'. Therefore he was afraid and did not abandon her, but as a census was then being held in Judaea, the first under Quirinius, he went up from Nazareth, where he was living, to Bethlehem, which was his native town, to be registered, for he was by descent of the tribe of Judah which used to live in that part of the country. Then he was ordered to leave for Egypt along with Mary and to stay there with the child until he should know, again by revelation, when to return to Judaea. At the birth of the child, then, in Bethlehem, since Joseph did not have any place to stay in that village, he put up in a cave near the village, and then while they were there Mary brought forth Christ and laid him in a manger, and this was where the wise men found him when they came from Arabia. I described to you how Isaiah announced beforehand about the sign referring to the cave (I said), and for the sake of those who have come today along with you I will recall the passage again (I said). And I recounted the passage from Isaiah which I have already set down, when I said that it is because of these utterances that

[1] Micah 5:2(1).

46

those who teach the mysteries of Mithras are prompted by the devil to say that it is in a place called by them a cave that their initiation ceremonies are enacted[1].

Well, the wise men from Arabia did not return to Herod, which he expected them to do, but according to their instructions departed to their own country by another way, and Joseph and Mary with the child, following the divine message, had already gone off to Egypt. So Herod was not able to recognize the child whom the wise men had come to worship, and ordered all the children in Bethlehem to be murdered indiscriminately. Even this incident was prophesied as destined to take place through Jeremiah; the Holy Spirit said these words: *A voice was heard in Ramah, mourning and great lamentation, Rachel mourning for her children, and she would not be comforted because they do not exist any longer*[2]. So because of this voice which was destined to be heard from Ramah, that is from Arabia (for there is even today a place called Ramah in Arabia), mourning was destined to overwhelm the place where Rachel, the wife of Jacob, who was called Israel, the holy patriarch, was buried, that is Bethlehem; the mothers were mourning for their own children who were murdered and had no comfort for the disaster which had befallen them. Further the text of Isaiah, *He will take the power of Damascus and the spoil of Samaria*[3], meant that the power of the evil demon who dwelt in Damascus would be conquered by Christ as soon as he was born. Now this evidently took place. The wise men, who had been forcibly carried away into all evil practices

[1]Notice that Justin has added to the account of Christ's birth in the gospels the details that the wise men came *from Arabia* and that the place where Christ was born was *a cave*. The first is certainly a guess of his own. The second just might be based on oral tradition picked up in Bethlehem.
[2]Jer. 38(31):15.
[3]Isa. 8:4.

which were operated by that demon, on coming to worship Christ appear to have been freed from that power which had exploited them, which the Word allegorically stated to dwell in Damascus. It is appropriate that it should figuratively call that power Samaria because it is sinful and unholy. But not even any of you can deny that Damascus was and is part of the land of Arabia, even if it is at the moment attached to Syrophoenicia[1]. So, my friends, it would be proper for you in a subject which you do not understand to learn from us Christians, who have received grace from God, and not to contend at every point that your doctrines must prevail, and so dishonour the acts of God ... "

[*There follows a quotation of Isa.* 29:13,14][2]

87. On my saying this, Trypho said: "From this on, do not regard me as putting the questions which I ask in an attempt to refute your arguments but as desiring information on the subject about which I enquire. [*Then he quotes Isa.*11:1-3.]

I grant you (he said) that these words are spoken of Christ. But you also say that he existed originally as God, and you say that he became incarnate according to the will of God and that he was born of the Virgin as a man. Now how can his pre-existence be demonstrated if he is filled with the powers of the Holy Spirit, which the Word lists through Isaiah, as if he originally lacked these powers?"

I answered: "You have asked a very intelligent and understanding question. It certainly does seem to be a difficulty. But listen to what I say so as to know the solution of the matter. The Word says that this list of powers of the Spirit

[1]This last clause is very odd, because there is evidence that Damascus was not added to Syrophoenicia until the reign of the Emperor Septimius Severus (192-211 A.D.), long after Justin's martyrdom. It is likely then that this clause was added very early in the history of the manuscript tradition by a scribe.
[2]Caps. 79-86 are omitted.

48

came upon him not because he was lacking in them, but because they are destined to achieve their rest in him, that is to reach finality in his case, so that there would be no more prophets according to the old tradition among your race. And this you can see with your own eyes, for after him no prophet at all has occurred among you. You can understand from my words that it was by each prophet receiving one or perhaps a second power from God that the prophets among you used to do and speak what we too learn from the Scriptures. Solomon, for instance, had the spirit of wisdom and Daniel of understanding and counsel, and Moses of might and godliness, and Elijah of fear and Isaiah of knowledge, and the others similarly had each one, or one power succeeding another alternately, as Jeremiah and the minor prophets and David and, in short, any others who were prophets among you. The Spirit therefore rested, that is it ceased, when he came, after whose coming those phenomena were meant to cease from among you, at the period when this divine policy of his dwelling among men was inaugurated. Yet also these phenomena achieved rest again in him as it was prophesied that gifts would be given which he gives from the grace of the power of that Spirit to those who believe in him, as he knows each to be worthy. I have already stated and I say again that it was prophesied that this development would occur by his means after his ascent into heaven.

[*There follow citations of Ps.* 67(68) : 19 *and Joel* 2:28,29(3:1,2).]

88. It is possible to see among us both women and men who have endowments from the Spirit of God. Therefore the prediction was made that the powers enumerated by Isaiah would come on him, not because he was lacking in power, but so that there would not be any more after him. It should be a proof of this for you that this event of which I told you took place, the arrival of the wise men from Arabia

who as soon as the child was born came and worshipped him. For even when he was only just born he possessed his power. He grew up according to the normal growth of all men, he used whatever means were suitable, supplied each stage of his growth with its proper material, ate every sort of food, and waited thirty years, more or less, until John appeared as a herald of his arrival and pioneered the way of baptism, as I have already shown. Then when Jesus came to the river Jordan, where John was baptizing, he went down into the water, and fire was kindled in the Jordan[1], and the apostles of this Christ of ours wrote that when he came up from the water the Holy Spirit perched upon him in the form of a dove. We know that he did not come to the river because he needed to be baptized or that the Spirit should come on him in the form of a dove, just as he did not endure the experience of birth and of crucifixion because he needed to do so; but he did this for the sake of the human race who ever since Adam's time had fallen under the power of death and of the serpent's deceit, as each person committed sin on his own responsibility. God wanted those who possessed free-will and power of self-direction, that is both angels and men, to do whatever he had given into the power of each to do; so he arranged that if they should choose to do what was pleasing to him he would preserve them immune from corruption and punishment, but if they behaved wickedly he would punish each as seemed best to him. Not even the fact that he sat on an ass when he entered Jerusalem, which was prophesied, as we have shown, conferred on him the power of being Christ, but he was giving an indication to men that he was Christ, just as at the incident of John's

[1]This, wholly unhistorical, detail is found added to the account of Jesus' Baptism in the apocryphal *Gospel according to the Hebrews*, and in several other apocryphal works, some of them with Gnostic associations.

baptism there had to be an indication for men so that they should know who was the Christ. But when John was sitting on Jordan's bank and preaching the baptism of repentance, and was wearing only a girdle made of hide and a garment of camel's hair, and ate nothing except locusts and wild honey, people thought that he was the Christ. He openly declared to them, 'I am not the Christ, but the voice of one who is crying aloud; for one more powerful than I will come whose sandals I am not worthy to carry.'[1] And Jesus came to the Jordan and was thought to be the son of Joseph the carpenter, and, as the Scriptures proclaimed, he looked *unlovely*[2], and was regarded as just a carpenter (when he lived among men he used to make these articles of carpentry, ploughs and yokes, in order to teach by this means the symbols of right living and an active life). Then the Holy Spirit, as I have already said, perched upon him in the form of a dove for the sake of these people, and a voice came from the heavens, *Thou art my son, this day have I begotten thee*[3]; the voice meant that his birth as far as men were concerned took place at the point from which it began to be known who he was."

89. Trypho said, "You can be sure that all our people are expecting the Christ, and, as you say, all the Scriptures speak about him; we admit this. And I acknowledge that the name Jesus (Joshua) has impressed me, for it was given to the son of Nun and also applies here[4]. But we doubt if

[1] A conflation of John 1:20,23 and Matt. 3:11.
[2] Isa. 53:2,3.
[3] Ps. 2:7; only a minority of manuscripts at Luke 3:23 give the Voice's utterance in this form; it is interesting to find Justin supporting this reading.
[4] The version of the name Joshua in the Septuagint is precisely the same as the Greek version of the name Jesus; the two are in Hebrew or Aramaic etymologically connected. This far from remarkable coincidence deeply impressed many of the writers of the early Church, including Justin, who uses it several times.

the Christ could have been crucified in this dishonourable way for *he who is crucified* is said in the law to be cursed[1], so that on that point I am most unwilling to be convinced. It is clear indeed that the Scriptures declare that the Christ is destined to suffer, but if it is to be through a form of suffering cursed in the law, we would like to know if you have any proofs on this point."

"If the Christ was not destined to suffer," I said to him, "and the prophets had not foretold that *he will be led to execution because of the lawless acts of the people* and *he will be dishonoured* and *will be scourged* and *will be numbered among the transgressors* and *will be led as a sheep to the slaughter*, and the prophet declares that *no one will be able to declare his race*[2], then there would be good reason for bewilderment. But if this prophecy is what delineates him and informs everybody, why should we not confidently believe in him? Whoever knows the writings of the prophets will say it is he, and nobody else, once they have heard that this man was crucified."

90. "Lead us too forward, then," he said, "by quoting the Scriptures so that we too may be convinced. We know indeed that the Christ suffers and *is destined to be led away like a sheep*[3]. But demonstrate to us whether he is also destined to be crucified and to die so shamefully and dishonourably a death which is cursed in the law. We cannot reach such a conception."

"I know," I said, "that what the prophets said and did, as has been admitted on your side, they concealed in figures and types so that most of their utterances are not easily understood by everybody, and they obscured the truth in them so that students have to take trouble to find and to learn."

[1]Deut. 21:23.
[2]Isa. 53: 8,3,4,12,7,8.
[3]Isa. 53:7.

They said, "We admitted this."

"Then," I said, "you should mark the consequence. Moses first indicated this thing which appeared to be a curse by the signs which he did."

"What signs do you mean?" he said.

"When the people were fighting against Amalek," I said, "and the Son of Nun, who was called by the name of Jesus (Joshua), was beginning the battle, Moses himself was praying to God, holding out his hands on each side of him. Hur and Aaron held them up the whole day long to prevent them falling down as he grew tired. If he modified this position which reproduces the cross, as it is written in the writing of Moses, *the people were defeated*; but if he continued in this posture Amalek was thus far conquered[1], and as long as he was strong he was strong by the cross. The people did not prevail because Moses was praying so much, but because, as the name of Jesus was in the beginning of the battle, Moses was making the sign of the cross. Which of you does not know that a prayer accompanied by grief and tears most of all propitiates God, and the prayer of one who is in a prone position and who kneels on his knees? But neither Moses himself nor anybody else after him prayed in this particular posture, seated on a stone. And indeed the stone has a symbolic meaning, referring to Christ, as I have said.

91. Further, God indicated the strength of the mystery of the cross in another passage. He spoke through Moses in the blessing with which he blessed Joseph:

[*There follows a quotation from Deut.* 33:13-17.]

Nobody could either say or show that the horns of the unicorn imply any other subject or pattern than the sign which indicates the cross. For there is one piece of wood which stands upright and the upper part of it stretches up

[1]Exod. 17:10-12.

53

into a horn when the cross-piece is fitted to it, and the ends appear on each side like horns joined to the original horn. And the piece of wood fitted into the middle, on which those who are crucified are seated, itself sticks out like a horn, and is itself fitted in and fixed with the other horns. And the text, *With them shall he butt nations together even at the end of the earth*[1] is prophetic of the events now taking place among all nations. Butted, that is to say pricked to the heart, men from all nations have been by means of this mystery converted to piety from futile idols and demons. And the same symbol acts in destruction and condemnation to the unbelievers, in the same way as, when the people left Egypt, by means of Moses stretching out his hands and the son of Nun being called by the name of Jesus (Joshua) Amalek was defeated and Israel victorious. Again, the public display made by the type and sign in the incident of the serpents biting Israel appears to have taken place for the salvation of those who believed that death was then predicted as destined to befall the serpent through him who was going to be crucified. Salvation was for those who had been bitten by the serpent and was for those who took refuge with him who sent his crucified Son into the world. The prophetic Spirit was not teaching us through Moses to believe in the serpent, since it indicates at the very beginning that he was cursed by God, and it indicates in Isaiah that he was due to be executed by the great sword . . . .[2]

94[3]. Tell me, was it not God who ordained through Moses that neither *image nor likeness* either of *the things in heaven above* nor of the things *on earth* should ever be made[4], and yet he *caused the brazen serpent to be made* in the desert

[1]Deut. 33:17.
[2]Num. 21:9; Gen. 3:14; Isa. 27:1.
[3]Caps. 92 and 93 are omitted.
[4]Exod. 20:4.

54

through Moses, and *set it up for a sign*[1], and by this sign those who had been bitten by serpents were healed, and God cannot be charged with doing wrong? He proclaimed a mystery by these means, as I have said already; he declared by this that he is dissolving the power of the serpent, who caused the sin done by Adam to come about, and to those who believe in him who was destined to be killed by this sign, that is by the cross, he declared salvation from the bites of the serpent, which are evil deeds, idolatry and other wrongdoing. If this interpretation is not given, supply me with a reason why Moses set up the brazen serpent as a sign and told those who were bitten to turn their eyes to it, and those who were bitten were healed, and yet this is the man who had given a command to make no image of any sort."

The second of the group who had arrived on the second day said, "What you say is true; we have no reason to give. Indeed, I have often asked the teachers about this point, and nobody gave me a reason. So continue with your argument, for we are interested in your explanation of a mystery in a subject which lays the doctrines of the prophets open to disparagement." I continued, "In the same way as God commanded the sign to take place by means of the brazen serpent and yet is not to be blamed, in just this way a curse attaches itself to crucified men in the law, and yet no curse is attached to God's Christ, through whom he saves all who have done things which deserve the curse.

95. In fact every member of the human race will be found liable to the curse according to the law of Moses; for it said *Cursed is every one who does not continue in the things written in the book of the law to do them*[2]. Even you would not dare to deny that nobody has scrupulously performed everything, but some have observed the ordinances more

[1]Num. 21:8,9.
[2]Deut. 27:26.

55

than others and some less. But if those who are under the law appear to be liable to this curse because they have not observed everything, will not the Gentiles appear to be far more liable to the curse, for they commit idolatry and homosexuality and indulge in other evil practices? So if the Father of the universe willed that his own Christ should take on himself the curses of all on behalf of men from every race, knowing that when he had been crucified and had died he would raise him up, why do you argue as if he who submitted to such suffering according to the Father's will was accursed, and not rather lament for yourselves? For even if his Father and he himself brought about his suffering of these things for the human race, it was not in obedience to the counsel of God that *you* did this; for when you murdered the prophets you were not practising true religion. Let none of you say, If the Father willed him to suffer in this way, so that *healing by his stripe*[1] should come to the human race, we have done nothing wrong. If indeed you produce this argument after repenting for your sinful acts and recognizing that this is the Christ and observing his commandments, I have already said that forgiveness of your sins will be available for you. But if you anathematize him and those who believe in him and murder them when you have the power to do so, how can punishment for having laid hands on him fail to be exacted from you as people who are in the wrong and sinners and altogether hard-hearted and devoid of understanding?

96. Further, the text in the law *Cursed is everyone who hangs on a tree*[2] nerves us to a hope which hangs upon the crucified Christ, for we do not believe that God cursed this crucified man, but rather that God foretold what you and people like you would do, for you did not understand that this man has existed before all things and is destined to be

[1] Isa. 53:5.
[2] Deut. 21:23.

56

the everlasting priest of God and King and Christ. It is open to you to see with your own eyes that this has taken place. You curse in your synagogues all those who have become Christians following him, and so do the other Gentiles who make this curse effective when they execute those who only confess themselves to be Christians. To both groups we say, *You are our brothers*[1], recognize instead the truth of God. And when neither you nor they are convinced by us, but attempt to force us to deny the name of Christ, we prefer rather to be put to death and we hold out, for we are convinced that God will give us all the rewards which he has promised through Christ. In addition, we pray for you that you may receive mercy from Christ. Christ taught us to pray for our enemies, saying, Be kind and pitiful, as your heavenly Father is, and indeed we do perceive that God almighty is kind and pitiful, for he causes the sun to rise on both the unthankful and the good and the rain to fall on the godly and on the wicked[2], though he has taught us that he will judge them all.

97. Notice that the fact that the prophet Moses remained until the evening, when *Hur and Aaron were holding up his hands*[3] in this posture, did not happen undesignedly. Notice that the Lord remained almost till evening upon the cross, and at evening they buried him; then he rose again on the third day. This was declared through David in this text: *I cried with my voice unto the Lord, and he heard me out of his holy hill. I laid me down and slept; I rose up again, because the Lord was my helper*[4]. Through Isaiah too a similar prophecy was made about him, concerning the manner in which he was destined to die, in this text: *I stretched out my hands to a*

[1]Isa. 66:5.
[2]Justin is apparently quoting a conflation of Luke 6:35 sq. and Matt. 5:45.
[3]Exod. 17:12.
[4]Ps. 3:5,6.

disobedient and gainsaying people, to those who went in a way which was not right[1]. And Isaiah himself said that he was going to rise again, *His grave was taken away from the midst*[2], and I will give *the rich in exchange for his death*[3]. And in other passages David spoke in an allegorical figure of his suffering and his cross, in those texts from the twenty-first (twenty-second) psalm: *They pierced my hands and my feet, they numbered all my bones, they observed me and looked on me. They parted my garments among them and on my raiment they cast lots*[4]. When they crucified him in the process of fixing in the nails they pierced his hands and his feet, and those who crucified him divided his garments among them, casting lots, each dividing what he wanted to choose according to the fall of the die. And yet you allege that this psalm was not spoken with reference to Christ because you are altogether purblind and do not understand that nobody who was called an anointed king in your race ever was pierced in his hands and feet while still alive and died by this mysterious sign, that is, by crucifixion, except this Jesus alone.

98. I would like to recite the whole psalm to you, so that you may learn of his piety towards the Father, and how he referred everything to him, and how he even asked to be saved from this death by him; I will also show in this psalm what sort of people were those who attacked him and demonstrate that he really did become a man capable of human sufferings."

[*There follows a quotation of Ps.* 21(22):2-24.]

99. When I recited this I went on, "I will demonstrate to you by this argument that the whole Psalm is to be referred to Christ, and by going through it again. The very

[1] Isa. 65:2.
[2] Isa. 57:2 (LXX).
[3] Isa. 53:9 (LXX).
[4] Ps. 21(22):2-5.

first words are, *My God, my God, hearken to me, why hast thou deserted me?*[1] This foretold of old what was destined to be said in the time of Christ. For when he was crucified he said, My God, my God, why hast thou forsaken me?[2] The next words are *The words of my offences are far from my salvation; my God, I will cry to thee by day and thou shalt not hearken, and by night and not for lack of my understanding*[3], so that what he was later to do was foretold. On the day on which he was going to be crucified he took three of his disciples to the hill which is called the hill of Olives, situated near to the Temple in Jerusalem, and he began to pray, saying, Father, if it is possible, let this cup pass from me. And next he prayed and said, Not as I will, but as thou willest[4], showing by these words that he really had become a man capable of suffering. And to prevent anybody saying 'So he did not know that he was destined to suffer!', he immediately adds in the psalm, *and not for lack of my understanding*, just as it was not a sign of lack of understanding in God that he asked the question, *Adam, where art thou?*, nor questioned Cain, *Where is Abel?*[5], but to prove what sort of a man each was, and so that the information should reach us by being written down. Similarly he gave this indication not for lack of his own understanding, but of the understanding of those who thought that he was not Christ but imagined that they could kill him and that he would remain in Hades like an ordinary man.

100. The text that follows, *And thou dwellest in the holy place, O thou worship of Israel*[6] indicated that he was going to do something worthy of praise and astonishment; he was

[1]Ps. 21(22):2.
[2]Matt. 27:46; Mk. 15:34.
[3]Ps. 21(22):2,3 (LXX).
[4]Matt. 26:39; Mk. 14:36.
[5]Gen. 3:9; 4:9.
[6]Ps. 21(22):4.

59

going to rise from the dead the third day after being crucified, a gift which he had received from his Father. I have shown that Christ is called both Jacob and Israel. And I have shown that mysterious predictions were made about him not only in the Blessing of Joseph and of Judah, but also it is written in the gospel, where he says, All things have been delivered to me by the Father, and no one knows the Father but the Son, nor the Son except the Father and those to whomsoever the Son reveals him[1]. He has therefore revealed to us whatever we understand from the Scriptures also through his grace, recognizing him as the first-born of God and before all created things, and also the descendant of the patriarchs, since he became incarnate through a Virgin of their race and submitted to become a man, *unlovely, dishonoured*[2], and subject to suffering. This is why among his utterances he said, when he was discoursing about his being destined to suffer, The Son of Man must suffer many things and be rejected by the Pharisees and scribes, and must be crucified and on the third day rise again[3]. He called himself Son of Man either because of his birth through the Virgin, who was, as I have said, of the race of David and Jacob and Isaac and Abraham, or because Abraham[4] himself was the father of those who have been mentioned, from whom Mary traced her descent, for we know that those who beget females are reckoned as the fathers of the children whom their daughters produce. Further, when one of his disciples, formerly called Simon, recognized him as Son of God, Christ, according to the revelation of his Father, he renamed him Peter. We find him described as Son of God in the memoirs of his apostles and we call him Son and perceive also that he

[1]Matt. 11:27; Luke 10:22.
[2]Isa. 53:2,3.
[3]Matt. 16:21; Mk. 8:31; Luke 9:22.
[4]Possibly a mistake for Adam.

existed before all created things and came forth from the Father by his power and wisdom. He also receives the title of Wisdom and Day and Dayspring and Sword and Stone and Rod[1] and Jacob and Israel in one way or another among the prophetic utterances, and he has become man through the Virgin, so that by the very channel whereby disobedience from the serpent took its starting-point, by this same channel it should receive its destruction. For Eve was a virgin and pure, but she conceived the word from the serpent and brought forth disobedience and death. But Mary the Virgin, receiving faith, and joy, when the angel Gabriel announced to her the good news that the Spirit of the Lord shall come upon her and the power of the Most High shall overshadow her, therefore that which is born of her is holy, the Son of God, answered: Let it be unto me according to thy word[2]. Through her was born this man through whom God is destroying the serpent and the angels and men who resemble him, and is operating release from death for those who repent of their evil acts and believe in him.

101. The next verses of the psalm are these where it is said: *Our fathers hoped in thee. They hoped and thou didst deliver them. They cried unto thee, and they were not ashamed. But I am a worm and no man, a very scorn of men and the outcast of the people*[3]. They indicate that he recognizes as fathers those people who put their hope in God and were saved by him, who were the ancestors of the Virgin through whom he was born when he became man, and he mentions that he himself will be saved by the same God, but he does not profess to do anything by his own wisdom or might. He made the same admission during his life on earth. When someone

---

[1]Prov.8:12 (Wisdom); Ps. 117(118):24 (Day); Zech. 6:12 (Dayspring); Isa. 27:1 (Sword); Dan. 2:34 (Stone); Isa. 11:1 (Rod).
[2]Luke 1:26,35.
[3]Ps. 21(22):5-7.

said to him, Good Lord, he answered, Why do you call me good? There is One good, my Father who is in heaven[1]. The words *I am a worm and no man, a very scorn of men and the outcast of the people* indicated what is evident and took place and happened to him. For we, the people who believe in him, are everywhere treated with *scorn*; *the outcast of the people* means that he was despised and dishonoured by your people and endured the sufferings which you inflicted on him. The words that follow next are, *All those who looked at me mocked me, and spoke with their lips and wagged their heads. He hoped in the Lord, let him deliver him, because he desires him*[2]. They predicted likewise that experiences like these would befall him. Those who saw him crucified each wagged his head and twisted their lips and curled their nostrils to each other and said sarcastically the same words which are written in the memoirs of the apostles: He called himself the Son of God; let him come down and walk; let God save him[3].

103. [*Next he quotes Ps.* 21(22): 11-15.]

This was likewise a prediction of what happened to him. For on that night when some of your people despatched by the Pharisees and scribes and conditioned by their teaching encountered him from the Mount of Olives they surrounded him and it is they whom the Word called calves, armed with horns and bent on destruction... The text *there is none to help*[4] is indicative also of what happened. Nobody, not a single one, appeared as an ally to aid him, guiltless though he was. And the text *They opened their mouth against me as a roaring lion*[5] indicates the man who was then the King of the Jews, who was also called Herod,

[1]Matt. 19:16 sq.; Mk. 10:17; Luke 18:18 sq.
[2]Ps. 21(22): 8,9.
[3]Matt. 27:40,42; Mk. 15:30-32; Lk. 23:35,37. Cap. 102 is omitted.
[4]Ps. 21(22):11.
[5]Ps. 21(22):13.

the successor of Herod who, when he was born, murdered all the children born in Bethlehem, at that time. He conjectured that somewhere among them there was the child about whom the wise men from Arabia told him when they arrived. But he did not know of the counsel of him who is stronger than anybody, that Joseph and Mary had been told to depart to Egypt, taking the child, and to remain there until it should be revealed to them again that they should return back to their own country. They departed and were there until the Herod who had killed the children in Bethlehem died and Archelaus succeeded him. And Archelaus died before Christ reached the point of fulfilling the divine policy which took place in his crucifixion according to the Father's will. Herod succeeded Archelaus and received the authority which was allotted to him[1]. It was to him that Pilate sent Jesus bound, anxious to do him a favour. God even foresaw that this would take place and spoke thus: *And they bore him off to the land of Assyria as a gift to the King*[2]. Alternatively he meant the devil by the roaring lion. Moses calls the devil a serpent, and in Job and Zechariah he is called devil, and is named *Satanas* by Jesus, indicating that he has gained a composite name from the practices which he follows. For *satan* in the language of the Jews and Syrians[3] means apostate, and the *nas* is a word for which the interpretation 'serpent'

[1]Justin is in error here. Herod Antipas did not succeed Archelaus; and Archelaus did not abandon his kingdom by death. Herod Antipas received one-third of the kingdom of his father Herod the Great, comprising Galilee and Peraea, and Archelaus received another third, comprising Judaea, and a third son of Herod the Great the remaining third. In 6 A.D., after the Jews had sent a deputation to the Roman senate complaining of Archelaus' misgovernment, the Romans deposed him. But Herod Antipas continued to govern his share of Herod the Great's original Kingdom, and it was of course from his territory that Jesus came.

[2]Hosea 10:6 (LXX). Perhaps we should read here, *They bound him and carried him off*.

[3]i.e. Aramaic.

is named. From both these words comes the single name *Satanas*. As soon as he had come up from the river Jordan, when the sentence was uttered, *Thou art my son, this day have I begotten thee*, it is recorded in the memoirs of the apostles that this devil encountered him and tempted him until the devil said Worship me, and Christ answered him, Get thee behind me, Satan; thou shalt worship the Lord thy God and him only shalt thou serve[1]. As he had led Adam astray, he imagined that he would be able to make some effect upon this man. Again, the text, *As water was poured out all my bones also were scattered, my heart became like melting wax in the middle of my belly*[2] was a prediction of what happened to him on that night when they went out against him at the Mount of Olives to arrest him. In the memoirs, which, I may say, were compiled by the apostles and those who were their immediate followers, it is written that sweat like drops of blood flowed down as he was praying and saying, Let this cup, if it be possible, pass from me. It is clear that his heart was trembling and so were his bones, and his heart was like wax melting into his belly, so that we should know that the Father willed that his own Son should for our sake really pass through these sufferings, and we should not say that because he was the Son of God he had no real share in what took place and what happened to him. The text *My strength is dried up as a potsherd and my tongue cleaves to my throat*[3], as I said, is a prediction of his silence; he made no reply on any point though he used to refute as unlearned all the teachers amongst you[4]. .

105. [*Next he quotes Ps.* 21(22):20-22.]

This too is instruction and prediction about his circumstances and what was to happen to him. I have already

[1]Matt. 4:10 and 16:23.
[2]Ps. 21(22):15.
[3]Ps. 21(22):15.
[4]Cap. 104 is omitted.

shown that this man was the only-begotten of the Father of the universe, begotten into individual existence from him as Word and Power[1], and later becoming man through the Virgin, as we have learnt from the memoirs. He similarly foretold that he was to die by crucifixion. The text, *Save my soul from the sword and my only-begotten from the paw of the dog; save me from the mouth of the lion and my weakness from the horns of the unicorns*[2] indicates likewise the sort of suffering by which he was to die, that is by crucifixion. I have already explained to you that the shape of *horns of the unicorns* is the shape of the cross only. His prayer that his soul should be saved *from the sword* and the *lion's mouth* and the *dog's paw* was a request that nobody should control his soul, so that when we come to depart this life we may make the same request to God who is able to turn aside every shameless and wicked angel to prevent him seizing our soul. I have shown you that our souls survive from the incident of Samuel's soul being summoned up by the ventriloquist woman at Saul's demand[3]. It appears that all the souls of those who were good men like Samuel and of the prophets had fallen under the authority of powers like those, as is indeed apparent from the facts themselves in the case of the ventriloquist. Consequently God teaches us through his Son to strive by all means to be good and at our departure to ask that our souls should not fall under a power of that character. Further when he gave up his spirit on the cross he said, *Father, into thy hands I commend my spirit*[4], as I have learnt from the memoirs. Again, he firmly directed his disciples towards their behaviour surpassing that of the Pharisees, and if not

[1]Or, with another reading, "having become a separate being", and this is perhaps preferable.
[2]Ps. 21(22):21,22 (LXX).
[3]1 Sam. 28:7,11,14.
[4]Luke 23:46.

they had to realize that they would not be saved; he is recorded in the memoirs as saying this: Unless your righteousness exceed the righteousness of the scribes and Pharisees, you shall not enter into the kingdom of heaven[1].

106. He trusted that his Father would supply him with everything that he wanted and would raise him from the dead. He urged all those who fear God to praise God for his having shown mercy to every race of men who are believers even by means of the mystery of this crucified man. He stood in the midst of his brethren, the apostles. After he had risen from the dead he convinced them that before his suffering he had told them that he must suffer these experiences and that they were predicted by the prophets. They were sorry for having deserted him when he was crucified, and accompanying them he sang praise to God, as is recorded as taking place in the memoirs of the apostles. All this the remainder of the psalm made clear. It runs thus: *I will declare thy name among my brethren, in the midst of the church will I praise thee. You who fear the Lord, praise him, glorify him, all you seed of Jacob; let all the seed of Israel fear him*[2]. The statement that he gave a new name, Peter, to one of the apostles, and it being recorded in his memoirs that this incident took place, along with his having called two other brothers, the sons of Zebedee, by the name of Boanerges (which means 'sons of thunder'), was all an indication that he was the same being through whom the name Jacob was given to him who was called Israel[3] and the name Joshua (Jesus) was given to Oshea; it was by the man of this name that the people who remained from those who had left Egypt was led into the land promised to the patriarchs.

[1]Matt. 5:20.
[2]Ps. 21(22):23,24.
[3]Justin has clearly made a slip here, as these two names should be transposed.

Moses revealed that the same man would rise as a star by means of the race of Abraham when he said *A star shall rise out of Jacob and a ruler out of Israel*[1]. And another text says *Behold a man, his name is Dayspring*[2]. So a star rose in heaven when he was born, as is written in the memoirs of the apostles. The wise men from Arabia, recognizing him from this sign, arrived and worshipped him.

107. Now, to prove that on the third day after he was crucified he was destined to rise from the dead: it is written in the memoirs of the apostles that the people of your race during an argument with him said 'Show us a sign.' He answered them, A wicked and adulterous generation seeks for a sign, and no sign shall be given to them except the sign of Jonah[3]. These words which he spoke were a secret intimation to be understood by those who heard him that after his crucifixion he would rise again on the third day. He was indicating that your generation was wickeder and more adulterous than the city of the Ninevites. When, after being vomited up on the third day from the belly of the great fish, Jonah announced to them that after three[4] days they would be destroyed all together, they declared a fast of every single living being, men and irrational beasts; they put on sackcloth, they lamented continually, they truly repented from their hearts and turned their backs on wickedness, they believed that God was compassionate and loving towards everybody who turned away from evil, so that even the king of that city and the nobles put on sackcloth with the rest and continued assiduously in fasting and supplication, and they obtained as a result the sparing of the city. Now when Jonah was grieved that the city was not destroyed on

[1]Num. 24:17.
[2]Zech. 6:12 (LXX).
[3]Matt. 16:4.
[4]Another mistake of Justin's; the number should be forty, but he is misled by his passion for spurious coincidence.

the third day, as he had announced, by divine agency a gourd sprang up for him, and he sat under it and received shade from the heat (this gourd was a miraculously fast-growing colocynth; Jonah had neither planted nor watered it but it spontaneously sprang up to provide shade for him); on the next day it was withered, and Jonah was annoyed at this, and God rebuked him for his unjustified annoyance at Nineveh's not being destroyed.

[*There follows a quotation of Jonah* 4:10,11.]

108. The men of your race all knew what had happened in Jonah's time. Christ had cried aloud amongst you that he would give you the sign of Jonah urging you even after his resurrection from the dead to repent for the evil deeds which you had done and to weep to God like the men of Nineveh so that your race and your city should not be overthrown and taken, as it was overthrown. Not only have you not repented when you heard that he had risen from the dead, but, as I have already said, you have appointed commissioners and sent them through the whole world to declare that 'An atheistic and lawless sect has been started by somebody called Jesus of Galilee, a fraud whom we crucified; but his disciples stole him by night from the tomb where he had been placed after the nails had been taken out and he had been removed from the cross, and they are deceiving people, alleging that he is risen from the dead and has ascended into heaven.' These commissioners assert against him that he taught the sort of practices of which you now accuse those who confess Christ as teacher and Son of God, practices which are atheistic and licentious and horrible in the eyes of the whole human race. In addition to this, though your city has been captured and your land laid waste you are not repenting, but you dare to curse him and all who believe in him. But we do not hate you and the people who are making insinuations of this sort against us

as a result of your propaganda; instead we pray that even now you may change your minds and receive mercy from God the Father of the universe who is full of compassion and overflowing with mercy."

VI. The Calling of the Gentiles: the Church.

(Justin is speaking)

117. "From of old God has been witnessing that all these sacrifices are pleasing to him which are offered through that name which Jesus Christ instituted, that is at the thanksgiving for the bread and the cup, which are celebrated by the Christians in every part of the earth. But he refuses the sacrifices which were celebrated by you and by those who were your priests, when he says: *I will not receive your sacrifices from your hands; for from the rising of the sun to its setting my name is glorified (he says), among the Gentiles, but you profane it*[1]. And even today you dispute the meaning of the passage and say that God did not receive the sacrifices of those who were then inhabiting Jerusalem and were called Israelites, but that he says that he was pleased by the prayers made by those men of that race who were then in the so-called Dispersion, and that he calls their prayers sacrifices. I agree indeed that prayers and thanksgivings offered by people who are worthy are the only sacrifices which are perfect and well-pleasing to God. These are the only sacrifices which Christians have been taught to make, and at the memorial of the solid and liquid food in which they recall the suffering which the Son of God suffered for their sakes. The chief priests and teachers of your race have caused his name to be profaned throughout the whole earth and to be blasphemed. These

[1]Malachi 1:10-12.

very accusations are the *filthy garments*[1] in which all those who from the name of Jesus have become Christians are clothed by you, but God will spectacularly remove them from us at the general resurrection, and one group he will place in his everlasting and indissoluble kingdom, incorruptible and immortal and untouched by grief; but the other group he will send away to the punishment of everlasting fire. But you and your teachers are deceiving yourselves when you imagine that the Word was speaking about those members of your race who were in the Dispersion, because he meant their prayers by *pure and pleasing sacrifices made in every place*[2]. You should realize that you are propagating falsehood and are attempting to deceive yourselves wholly, because in the first place not even today does your race exist *from the rising of the sun to its setting*, but there are nations among whom nobody of your race has ever lived. But there is no single race of men whatever, neither uncivilized nor civilized, nor called by any name of any sort, gypsies nor people called nomads[3], nor *cattle-drovers who live in tents*[4], in which prayers and thanksgivings are not addressed to the Father and Creator of the universe through the name of this crucified Jesus. Secondly, at the time when the prophet Malachi made this utterance your Dispersion was not yet throughout all the earth, as far as it now extends, as is clear from the Scriptures. . .[5] .

118. This is the chosen priest and everlasting king, the Christ, as Son of God. Do not imagine that Isaiah or the other prophets declared that at his Second Coming sacrifices of blood or of libations will be offered on an altar, but true and spiritual praises and thanksgivings. We have not

[1]Zech. 3:3.
[2]Mal. 1:11.
[3]Literally 'cart-dwellers nor people called homeless'.
[4]Gen. 4:20.
[5]Cap. 118:1-2a is omitted.

believed in him in vain, nor have we been deceived by those who taught us to do this, but this has happened by a wonderful providence of God so that we should turn out to be wiser and more pious than you who are religious and wise in imagination but not in fact, through the new calling and the eternal covenant, that is Christ's. It was in amazement at this that Isaiah said *And kings shall shut their mouth*; *because they to whom no announcement has been made shall see, and people who have not heard*[1]. *Lord, who has believed our report, and to whom has the arm of the Lord been revealed?*"[2] When I said this I added, "Trypho, I am trying, as far as possible, to state the same arguments over again, for the sake of those who arrived with you today, but briefly and concisely."

In reply he said, "You are doing well, and even if you repeat the same arguments at length, you can be sure that I and my companions will be glad."

119. I said, continuing, "My friends, do you imagine that we could have perceived these truths in the Scriptures if we had not received grace to perceive them by the will of him who willed them?

[*There follows a quotation of Deut.* 32:16-23.]

After that Righteous One had been murdered we grew up as another race and we shot forth like new and flourishing ears of corn, as the prophets said, *And many nations shall take refuge with the Lord in that day, and they shall make their dwelling in the midst of the earth*[3]. But we are not only a people but a holy people, as I have shown already, *And they shall call it a holy people, ransomed by the Lord*[4]. Therefore we are no contemptible assembly, not an uncivilized mob nor like the

---

[1] We should probably add after this clause, with the Septuagint "shall understand".
[2] Isa. 52:15-53:1.
[3] Zech. 2:11(15).
[4] Isa. 62:12.

nations of the Carians or Phrygians, but God chose us and *became manifest to those who had not sought him*, and *he said Behold I am God! to a nation which had not called upon my name*[1]. This is that nation which God of old promised to Abraham, and he promised to *make him a father of many nations*[2], not meaning nations of Arabians or Egyptians or Idumaeans; indeed Ishmael became father of a great nation (in this sense) and so did Esau, and there is now a great number of Ammonites. Noah was father of Abraham himself and in fact of the whole human race, and others have been ancestors of other races. What greater gift then does Christ graciously give to Abraham? This, that he called him by the voice of the same calling, saying *Go out of the land in which you are dwelling*[3]. And he calls us all by this same voice, and we have gone out now from the way of life in which we were living according to the custom of the rest of the inhabitants of the earth, an evil way of life. And we shall inherit the holy land with Abraham, when we receive the inheritance destined for the everlasting age, being children of Abraham through the same faith. Just as he believed the voice of God and *it was reckoned to him for righteousness*[4], in the same way we also have believed until we die the voice of God which was spoken again through the apostles of Christ and had been declared through the prophets, and we have turned our back on the things of the world. To Abraham then was promised a race which should have the same faith, pious and righteous, but not you, *in whom there is no faith*[5]..."

121[6]. As they kept silence, I went on: "The Word speaking through David about this Christ did not say that

[1] Isa. 65:1.
[2] Gen. 17:5.
[3] Gen. 12:1.
[4] Gen. 15:6.
[5] Deut. 32:20.
[6] Cap. 120 is omitted.

72

the nations would be blessed in his seed, but in him. The text runs thus: *His name is for everlasting; he shall rise higher than the sun and in him shall all the nations be blessed*[1]. If all nations are blessed in Christ and we who are men of all nations believe in him, then he is the Christ, and we are the people blessed through him. *God originally gave the sun*[2] to be worshipped, as it is written, and it is impossible ever to see anybody enduring as far as death for his faith in the sun. But people of every race of men can be seen both having endured in the past and now enduring through the name of Jesus so as to suffer any ill-treatment rather than deny him. For the Word of truth and wisdom is more fiery and more resplendent than the powers of the sun, and it enters into the depths of the heart and the mind. This is why the Word said *His name shall rise above the sun*. And again Zechariah says *His name is Dawn*[3]. And he speaks about him when he says, *Tribe by tribe they shall mourn*[4]. But if he was so resplendent and powerful at his First Coming in humbleness and unloveliness and contempt so that he fails to receive recognition among no race and from everybody induces repentance from the former evil way of life of each race, so that demons are subject to his name and all the powers and principalities fear the name of this man more than any in the past, will he not at his glorious Second Coming wholly destroy all who hate him and those who have wrongfully deserted him, but will give rest to his own and give to them all the things they have been longing for? To us therefore it has been given to hearken and to understand and to be saved through this Christ and to know all the counsel of the Father. This is why the Father said to

[1] Ps. 71(72): 17.
[2] Deut. 4:19.
[3] Zech. 6:12.
[4] Zech. 12:12.

him, *It is a great thing for thee to be called my servant, to restore the tribes of Jacob and to gather the Dispersion of Israel. I have made thee a light of the Gentiles, so that thou shouldest be for their salvation to the end of the earth*[1].

122. You think that this verse refers to the Strangers and Proselytes[2], but it is in fact spoken to us who have been enlightened through Jesus. For surely Christ could have borne witness to them, but as it is you are, as he said, twice as much sons of hell[3]. Neither are the utterances made through the prophets addressed to those classes of people, but to us; and the Word says about us, *I will lead the blind by a way which they have not known, they shall tread paths with which they are not acquainted. And I am a witness, says the Lord God, and my servant whom I have chosen*[4]. To whom does Christ bear witness? Clearly, to those who have believed in him. But the proselytes not only do not believe, but they blaspheme against his name twice as much as you do, and they are anxious to murder and maltreat us who believe in him; they are eager to be like you in everything. Again elsewhere he cries aloud: *I, the Lord, have called thee in righteousness, and I will hold thy hand and will strengthen thee, and I will make thee a covenant of the people, a light of the Gentiles, to open the eyes of the blind, to deliver the fettered from their chains*[5]. These things, my friends, were addressed to Christ and were about the Gentiles being enlightened. Or do you still insist upon saying that they were addressed to the law and the proselytes?"

[1] Isa. 49:6.
[2] i.e. Those Gentiles who had attached themselves to synagogues and read the Old Testament (literally "God-fearers"), and those who had been Gentiles but who had received circumcision and full initiation as proselytes.
[3] Perhaps Matt. 23:15.
[4] Isa. 42:16; 43:10.
[5] Isa. 42:6,7.

And some of those who had arrived on the second day shouted as if they were in a theatre, "Why not? Is he not speaking to the law and to those who were enlightened by it? These are the proselytes."

"No," I said, looking at Trypho. "For if the law had the power of enlightening the Gentiles and those who observed it, what was the need of a new covenant? But since God announced beforehand that he was going to institute *a new covenant* and *an everlasting law*[1] and ordinance, we shall not interpret it as the old law and its proselytes but as Christ and his proselytes, we Gentiles whom he enlightened, just as he says: *Thus says the Lord: In an acceptable time have I heard thee, and in a day of salvation have I succoured thee, and I have made thee a covenant of the Gentiles to establish the earth and to inherit the deserts as an inheritance*[2]. What is Christ's inheritance? Is it not the Gentiles? What is the covenant of God? Is it not Christ? Similarly he says elsewhere, *Thou art my son, this day have I begotten thee. Ask of me, and I shall give thee the Gentiles for thine inheritance, and the limits of the earth as thy possession*"[3].

VII. Conclusion: Summary; Some Objections Met; the Dialogue Ends.

(Justin is speaking)

127. "And other statements like these appear in the Lawgiver and in the prophets. I think I have said enough. Surely, when my God says *God went up from Abraham*, or *The Lord spoke to Moses*, or *The Lord went down to see the tower which the sons of men had built*, or *God shut Noah into*

[1] Jer. 38(31):31,33.
[2] Isa. 49:8.
[3] Ps. 2:7,8.

the ark[1], you did not think that the unoriginated God himself came down or went up anywhere? The ineffable Father and Lord of all does not come anywhere nor walk nor sleep nor rise up, but in his own place, wherever it is, he remains, seeing piercingly and hearing piercingly, without eyes and without ears but with inexpressible power. He surveys everything and knows everything, and not one of us escapes his notice. He is not moved, but he is incomprehensible by space and by the whole world, indeed he existed even before the world did. How could a being like this speak to anyone or become visible to anyone or appear on the smallest part of the earth? Why, the people on Sinai could not endure to look at the glory of him who was sent from him, nor could Moses endure to go into the tent which he had made, if it was filled by the glory from God, nor could the priest endure to stand before the temple when Solomon brought the ark into the house in Jerusalem which Solomon himself had built! Neither Abraham nor Isaac nor Jacob nor any other human being saw the Father and ineffable Lord of every single thing, and of Christ himself, but they saw him who was God according to the will of the Father, his Son, and his Angel (because he served his purpose). He determined that he should become man through the Virgin; he also on one occasion became fire at that conversation with Moses from the bush. Unless we interpret the Scriptures in this way, it will follow that the Father and Lord of the universe ceased to be in the heavens on the occasion when it was recorded through Moses: *And the Lord rained fire and brimstone out of heaven from the Lord on Sodom*, and again when through David this statement is made: *Lift up your gates, ye rulers, and be elevated, ye everlasting gates, and the King of glory shall go in*, and again when he says, *The Lord said unto my Lord,*

[1] Gen. 17:22; Exod. 6:29; Gen. 11:5; Gen. 7:6.

Sit thou on my right hand, until I make thine enemies the footstool of thy feet[1].

(*Justin is speaking*)

138. "You know, my friends, then," I said, "that it is said in Isaiah by God to Jerusalem, *I saved thee at Noah's flood*[2]. What God means by this is that the mystery of men being saved occurred at the Flood. Righteous Noah with the other people at the Flood, that is his wife and his three sons and his sons' wives, eight persons in number, were a sign of the number of the eighth day, on which Christ appeared after rising from the dead, a day which is however always first in power. For Christ, the first-born of all creation, also became the beginning of a new race, a race regenerated by him through water and faith and wood which includes the mystery of the cross, just as Noah was saved on a piece of wood as he rode on the waves with his family. When therefore the prophet said, *In the time of Noah I saved you*, he was equally addressing the people who were faithful to God and had these symbols. Further, Moses led your people through the sea holding a (wooden) rod in his hand. You think that God spoke only to your nation, or to the earth. Yet because, as the Scripture says, the whole earth was flooded, and the *water rose fifteen cubits*[3] above the mountains, God apparently did not speak to the earth but to the people obedient to him, for whom he had prepared a rest in Jerusalem through all the symbols associated with the Flood. I have said that those who had already been prepared through water and faith and wood and who repented for what they had sinfully done will escape the judgment of God which is destined to come[4]...

[1]Gen. 19:24; Ps. 23(24):7; Ps. 109(110):1.
[2]Isa. 54:8,9.
[3]Gen. 7:19,20.
[4]Caps. 139 and 140 are omitted.

77

141. I want to prevent you arguing that Christ was destined to be crucified, or that among your race there were destined to be some evildoers, and it could not have been otherwise. So I forestalled you and said briefly that God wanted angels and men to follow his purpose and decided to create them with freewill to do what is right, endowed with reason so that they could understand by whom they were given existence and through whose agency they came into being out of nothingness, and placed under a law so that they were to be judged by him if they behaved in a way contrary to right principle. We, men and angels, will be condemned if we do wrong for our own behaviour, unless we first alter our conduct. But if the Word of God records beforehand that some angels and men will certainly be punished, because he foresaw that they would be unalterably wicked, he predicted these events, but not because God caused them to be wicked. So, if they repent, everyone who wishes to gain mercy from God is able to do so and the Word pronounces them blessed, saying *Blessed is the man, unto whom the Lord imputeth no sin*[1]. This means, he who repents for his sins and receives forgiveness of sins from God, but not, as you and some others who resemble you in this say, deceiving yourselves, that even if people are sinners, but know God, the Lord will not impute sin to them. As proof of this we have the first sin of David which took place because of his boasting; it was forgiven when he had lamented and mourned as deeply as is recorded. If forgiveness was not given to a man of this sort before repentance, but this great king and anointed one and prophet wept and acted so drastically, how can those who are unclean and utterly desperate entertain hope that the Lord will not impute sin to them—unless they mourn and lament and repent? And,

[1]Ps. 31(32):2.

my friends", I said, "this single act of sin by David with Uriah's wife shows that when the patriarchs had several wives they did not do so as committing fornication but all their conduct was enacted as a piece of divine policy and as a series of mysteries. If it were to be acceptable that one should take whatever wives one liked, in whatever way, and to whatever number, one liked (which is the practice of the men of your nation in every country; both where they live and where they have emigrated they take women under the name of marriage), it would be much more acceptable that David should do this."

So when I had said this, my dearest friend Marcus Pompeius, I finished.

142. Trypho remained silent for some time, and then said: "You perceive that it was not deliberately that we met together in this discussion. I confess that I enjoyed the encounter greatly, and I know that my companions feel as I do. We found more than we expected or than we once thought it possible to expect. We would gain even more advantage if it was possible for us to do this more often, and examine the same arguments. But (said he) since you are about to make a journey by sea and are expecting daily to sail, do not hesitate if you go away to think of us as your friends."

"If I were to stay here," I said, "I would for my own sake like the discussion to take place every day. But I am even now expecting to sail, as God permits me and assists me, so I urge you to undertake this great struggle for your own salvation and be eager to choose the Christ of the almighty God rather than your own teachers."

After that we parted. They wished me for the future a safe journey and preservation from all evil. When I gave them my good wishes, I said, "I cannot pray any better prayer for you, my friends, than that you may recognize that every man is granted the opportunity of happiness through this religion, and that you may resolutely become what we are, recognizing that Jesus is the Christ of God."[1]

[1]This translation follows an emendation of the text which is otherwise difficult to make any sense of.